RATIONAL EMOTIVE
BEHAVIOURAL COUNSELLING
IN ACTION

SAGE COUNSELLING *IN ACTION*

Series Editor: WINDY DRYDEN

Sage Counselling in Action is a series of short, practical books developed especially for students and trainees. As accessible introductions to theory and practice, they have become core texts for many courses, both in counselling and other professions such as nursing, social work, education and management. Books in the series include:

Sue Culley and Tim Bond
Integrative Counselling Skills in Action, Second Edition

Windy Dryden and Michael Neenan
Rational Emotive Behavioural Counselling in Action, Third Edition

Michael Jacobs
Psychodynamic Counselling in Action, Third Edition

Diana Whitmore
Psychosynthesis Counselling in Action, Third Edition

Patricia D'Ardenne and Aruna Mahtani
Transcultural Counselling in Action, Second Edition

Ian Stewart
Transactional Counselling in Action, Second Edition

Dave Mearns and Brian Thorne
Person-Centred Counselling in Action, Second Edition

Petrūska Clarkson
Gestalt Counselling in Action, Third Edition

Tim Bond
Standards and Ethics for Counselling in Action, Second Edition

Peter Trower, Windy Dryden and Andrew Casey
Cognitive Behavioural Counselling in Action

RATIONAL EMOTIVE
BEHAVIOURAL COUNSELLING
IN ACTION
Third Edition

Windy Dryden *and*
Michael Neenan

SAGE Publications
London ● Thousand Oaks ● New Delhi

First edition published as *Rational-Emotive Counselling in Action*
in 1990, reprinted 1992, 1993, 1994, 1996, 1998
Second edition published 1999
Third edition published 2004

SAGE Publications Ltd
1 Oliver's Yard
55 City Road
London EC1 1SP

SAGE Publications Inc.
2455 Teller Road
Thousand Oaks, California 91320

SAGE Publications India Pvt Ltd
B-42, Panchsheel Enclave
Post Box 4109
New Delhi 110 017

British Library Cataloguing in Publication data

A catalogue record for this book is available from the British
Library

ISBN 0 4129 0212 6
ISBN 0 4129 0213 4 (pbk)

Library of Congress Control Number available

Typeset by M Rules
Printed in Great Britain by The Cromwell Press Ltd, Trowbridge, Wiltshire

Contents

Preface

Our goal in this book has been to present the essence of rational emotive behavioural counselling (REBC) *in action*. To this end we have structured the book in three parts. In Part 1, we outline the basic theoretical and practical principles of REBC. In Part 2, we detail a sequence of six steps that you need to follow when attempting to help your client with any given problem using REBC. Finally, in Part 3, we consider the process of rational emotive behavioural counselling from beginning to end. To highlight rational emotive behavioural counselling *in action* we have presented the case of Paula (a pseudonym) whom you will meet in Parts 2 and 3 of the book.

Windy Dryden, and Michael Neenan
April 2004

Part 1

THE BASIC PRINCIPLES OF RATIONAL EMOTIVE BEHAVIOURAL COUNSELLING

In this first part of the book we will first consider the theoretical under-pinnings of rational emotive behavioural counselling and then focus on the key practical elements of this counselling approach.

Theoretical Underpinnings of Rational Emotive Behavioural Counselling

Historical Context

Rational Emotive Behaviour Therapy (REBT) was originated in 1955 by Albert Ellis, a New York clinical psychologist. Ellis originally worked as a psychoanalyst and, while he enjoyed practising this mode of therapy, he later became dissatisfied with it because it was, in his words, 'inefficient' in that it took a long time and did not produce very effective therapeutic results. For a while Ellis experimented with the shorter-term psychoana-lytic psychotherapy and with various eclectic approaches before he founded REBT. In doing so he was influenced more by philosophers than by psychologists, returning to a long-standing interest in practical approaches within the philosophic tradition. In particular he was influ-enced by the views of Epictetus, a Roman philosopher, who stated that 'men are disturbed not by things but by their views of things'.

At that time in the mid-1950s most therapists were influenced by psy-choanalytic theories and methods and thus, to emphasise the logical and cognitive disputing aspects of his therapeutic approach, Ellis called his method 'rational therapy'. This caused problems in that it was generally assumed that rational therapy only involved a focus on cognition (that is, thoughts and beliefs). However, right from the start Ellis held that cognition, emotion, and behaviour were interrelated psychological processes and that his approach to therapy emphasised all three. In order to counter further unwarranted criticisms that were made about rational therapy, namely that it neglected emotion, Ellis retitled his approach to psychotherapy 'rational-emotive therapy' in 1961, a point which was stressed in the title of Ellis's first major book on RET (as the approach came to be known), entitled *Reason and Emotion in Psychotherapy* (Ellis, 1962). In 1993, Ellis changed the name of the therapy to Rational Emotive Behaviour Therapy (REBT) because he argued that commentators were neglecting its behavioural elements. This was never true of the therapy, and from the outset, in addition to focusing on clients' emotions and beliefs, rational emotive behavioural counsellors encourage their clients actively to put into practice what they learn in therapy through the use of behavioural methods (Ellis, 1994).

Goals, Purposes and Rationality

According to REBC theory humans are happiest when they set up important life goals and purposes and actively strive to achieve these. In doing so, we had better acknowledge that we live in a social world and thus we are encouraged to develop a philosophy of enlightened self-interest. This involves pursuing our valued goals while demonstrating what Alfred Adler called social interest – a commitment both to helping others achieve their valued goals and to making the world a socially and environmentally better place in which to live.

Given that we tend to be goal-directed, *rational* in REBC theory 'means primarily that which helps people to achieve their basic goals and purposes', whereas irrational 'means primarily that which prevents them from achieving these goals and purposes' (Dryden, 1996: 306). While rationality is not defined in any absolute sense, it does have four major criteria: namely, it is (a) flexible and non-extreme; (b) pragmatic; (c) logical; and (d) reality-based. Thus, a more extended definition of rationality would be, first, that which is flexible and non-extreme; secondly, that which helps people to achieve their basic goals and purposes; thirdly, that which is logical; and fourthly, that which is empirically consistent with reality. Conversely, an extended definition of irrationality would be, first, that which is rigid and non-extreme; secondly, that which prevents people from achieving their basic goals and purposes; thirdly, that which is illogical; and fourthly, that which is empirically inconsistent with reality.

Responsible Hedonism

REBC theory argues that as humans we are basically hedonistic in the sense that we seek to stay alive and to achieve a reasonable degree of happiness. Here hedonism does not mean 'the pleasures of the flesh' but involves the concept of personal meaning; a person can be said to be acting hedonistically when she is happy acting in a way that is personally meaningful for her. The concept of responsible hedonism means once again that we are mindful of the fact that we live in a social world and that ideally our personally meaningful actions should help to make the world a better place in which to live, or at the very least should not unduly harm anyone.

REBC theory makes an important distinction between short- and long-range hedonism. We are likely to be at our happiest when we succeed in achieving both our short-term and our long-term goals. Frequently, however, we defeat ourselves by attempting to satisfy our short-term goals while at the same time sabotaging our long-term goals. Thus, for example, we often strive to avoid discomfort when it would be advisable for us to experience discomfort because doing so would help us to achieve our long-term goals. Rational emotive behavioural counsellors encourage their clients to achieve a balance between the pursuit of their short- and long-range goals, while being mindful of the fact that what represents a healthy balance for a given person is best judged by that person.

Enlightened Self-interest

REB counsellors have often been accused of advocating selfishness since they actively encourage their clients to pursue happiness. However, this criticism is not accurate if we define selfishness as 'the ruthless pursuit of one's goals while cynically disregarding the goals and viewpoints of others'. Rather, REB counsellors encourage their clients to demonstrate enlightened self-interest (or healthy self-care), which involves putting themselves first most of the time while putting others, and particularly significant others, a close second. Enlightened self-interest also sometimes involves putting the desires of others before our own, particularly when the welfare and happiness of these others are of great importance to them and our desires are not primary. Self-sacrifice is discouraged unless the person wants to sacrifice herself and finds personal meaning and happiness in doing so.

Philosophic and Scientific Emphasis

Rational emotive behavioural theory stresses that we are born philosophers. We have the ability to think about our thinking and to realise that we are highly influenced by our implicit philosophies of life which are either flexible and undogmatic or musturbatory and absolutist. REBC theory agrees with the ideas of George Kelly (1955) that we are also scientists and are able to appreciate that our philosophies are basically hypotheses about ourselves, other people, and the world, which need to be tested. This is best done together with our philosophical abilities, particularly our ability to think critically about the logical and illogical aspects of our thought.

While Ellis (1976) has argued that humans have a strong tendency to think and act irrationally, he has stressed that we also have the ability to think critically about our thinking and behaviour and to correct the illogicalities in our thinking as well as to judge whether or not our hypotheses are consistent with reality. Rational emotive behavioural theorists do, however, appreciate that reality cannot be judged in any absolute manner but is best regarded as accurate if it is seen as such by a group of neutral observers (the principle of consensual reality).

Humanistic Outlook

REBC is not only philosophical and scientific in orientation but it takes a specific humanistic-existential approach to human problems and their solutions. This view conceptualises humans as holistic, indivisible, goal-directed organisms who have importance in the world just because we are human and alive. It encourages us to accept ourselves unconditionally with our limitations while at the same time encouraging us to work towards minimising our limitations. REBC agrees with the position of ethical humanism which 'encourages people to live by rules emphasising human interests over the interests of inanimate nature, of lower animals or of any assumed natural order or deity' (Ellis, 1980: 327). However, this does not mean being ecologically or environmentally insensitive, advocating the mindless slaughter of animals or being disrespectful of others' religious views. Furthermore, this outlook acknowledges that we are human and are in no way superhuman or subhuman.

Two Basic Biologically Based Tendencies

Rational emotive behavioural theory hypothesises that as humans we have a biologically based tendency to think irrationally as well as a similar tendency to think rationally. It thus differs from other approaches to counselling in emphasising the power of these biologically based tendencies over the power of environmental conditions to affect human happiness, although it by no means neglects the contribution of these environmental conditions to influence human emotion and behaviour. The view that irrational thinking is largely determined by biological factors, albeit always interacting with influential environmental conditions, rests on the seeming ease with which humans think crookedly and the prevalence of such thinking even among those humans who have been rationally raised. Ellis has noted in this regard that 'even if everybody had had the most rational upbringing, virtually all humans would often irrationally transform their individual and social preferences into absolutistic demands on (a) themselves (b) other people and (c) the universe around them' (Ellis, 1984a: 20).

Two Fundamental Human Disturbances

Ellis has noted that human psychological problems can be loosely divided into two major categories: ego disturbance and discomfort disturbance. Ego disturbance relates to the demands that we make about ourselves and the consequent negative self-ratings that we make when we fail to live up to our self-imposed demands. Furthermore, ego-disturbance issues may underpin what at first glance appear to be demands made of others or of life conditions. Thus, I may be angry at you because you are acting in a way which I perceive as a threat to my 'self-esteem'. The fact that my anger is directed outwardly towards you serves in this way to protect my own 'shaky self-esteem'.

Discomfort disturbance, on the other hand, is more related to the domain of human comfort and occurs when we make dogmatic commands that comfort and comfortable life conditions must exist.

As will be shown later in this part of the book, the healthy alternative to ego disturbance rests on a fundamental attitude of unconditional self-acceptance where a person fully accepts herself as a human being and who cannot be given a single global rating. The healthy alternative to discomfort disturbance rests on a philosophy of a high frustration or discomfort tolerance where we are prepared to tolerate frustration or discomfort, not for its own sake, but as a way of overcoming obstacles to the pursuit of our basic goals and purposes.

Psychological Interactionism

Rational emotive behavioural theory states that a person's thoughts, emotions and actions cannot be treated separately from one another. Rather, they are best conceptualised as being overlapping or interacting psychological processes. This is the principle of psychological interactionism. Thus, when we think about something we have a tendency to have an emotional reaction towards it and also a tendency to act towards it in some way. Also, if we have a feeling about a person then we are likely to have some thought about him and also, again, a tendency to act towards him in a certain manner. Similarly, if we act in a certain manner this is often based on my thoughts and feelings towards either an object or a person.

REBC is perhaps best known for the emphasis that it places on cognition and for its cognitive restructuring components. While it is true that it does emphasise the power of cognition in human happiness and disturbance, it does so while fully acknowledging the affective and behavioural components of human functioning. It stresses that these three fundamental human psychological processes almost always interact and often in complex ways (Ellis, 1985). Similarly, while the practice of rational emotive behavioural counselling is perhaps known for its cognitive restructuring methods, these are by no means the sole ingredients of the approach and REB counsellors frequently use emotive-evocative and behavioural methods to encourage clients to change their thinking.

REBC and Constructivism

While some critics (e.g. Mahoney, 1988) have argued that REBC is a rationalist approach to counselling and psychotherapy (i.e. that it holds that there is an objective reality and that people should be helped to view this reality), Ellis (1989) has argued that in fact REBC is a constructivist counselling approach. Thus, REBC theory holds that while people may well be influenced by their culture and family groups to have certain preferences, they construct rigid demands about their preferences. Indeed, as will be shown later, REBC theory does not have an elaborate viewpoint about how people acquire their disturbances, arguing that people bring their tendencies to construct demands and other irrational beliefs to their experiences, which other theories might argue cause them to be disturbed.

Where REBC as a constructivist approach to counselling differs from other constructivist approaches is in its position that some constructions are better for the individual than other constructions. Thus, it argues that some constructions can be clearly seen as unempirical, illogical and self-defeating (e.g. where a person constructs a belief that she is a failure for having failed an important exam). Conversely, REBC theory holds that other alternative constructions are more empirical, sensible and self-enhancing (e.g. when that same person constructs a belief that failing the exam only proves that she is a fallible human being who can both succeed and fail, but cannot be defined by either experience).

Thus, REB counsellors encourage their clients to take responsibility for their constructions and help them to stand back and view these constructions and change them when they are clearly unempirical, illogical and self-defeating. Furthermore, REB counsellors are explicit about the therapeutic constructions that they bring to the practice of counselling, inviting (but not demanding) their clients to share these constructions.

The ABC Framework

The ABC framework is the cornerstone of REBC practice and therefore merits detailed attention. There are, in fact, two different types of A in REBT. The first, known as the 'Situational A' refers to an objective description of what occurred in the situation in which the person disturbed himself. The second is known as the 'Critical A' and refers to the subjective aspect of the situation about which the person disturbed himself. Most frequently, a Critical A involves an inference about what happened in the Situational A.

B stands for beliefs. These are evaluative cognitions or constructed views of the world which are either rigid or flexible and extreme or non-extreme. When these beliefs are rigid they are called *irrational beliefs* and take the form of musts, absolute shoulds, have to's, got to's and so on. When your clients adhere to such rigid beliefs they will also tend to make irrational conclusions from these irrational premises. These irrational conclusions are extreme and take the form of: (a) *awfulising* – meaning more than 100 per cent bad, worse than it absolutely should be; (b) *low frustration tolerance* – meaning that your clients believe that they cannot envisage enduring situations or having any happiness at all if what they demand must not exist actually exists; and (c) *depreciation* – here your clients will depreciate themselves, other people, and/or life conditions.

When your client's beliefs are flexible they are called *rational beliefs* in REBC. Flexible beliefs often take the form of desires, wishes, wants, and preferences, which your clients do *not* transform into dogmatic musts, shoulds, oughts, and so on. When your clients adhere to such flexible rational beliefs they will tend to make rational conclusions from these rational premises. These conclusions are non-extreme and take the form of (a) *anti-awfulising* – here, for example, your clients will conclude 'it's bad, but not terrible' rather than 'it's awful' when faced with a negative event; (b) *high frustration tolerance* – here your clients may say 'I don't like it, but I can bear it'; and (c) *acceptance* – here your clients will accept themselves and other people as fallible human beings who cannot legitimately be given a single global rating. Also your clients will accept the world and life conditions as complex, composed of good, bad, and neutral elements, and thus will also refrain from giving the world a global rating.

C in the ABC framework stands for emotional, behavioural and thinking consequences of your client's beliefs about A. In REBC, the C's that follow from irrational beliefs about negative A's will be disturbed and are called unhealthy negative consequences, and C's that follow from rational beliefs about negative A's will be non-disturbed and are termed healthy negative consequences (Ellis, 1994). Unhealthy negative emotions are unhealthy for any one or more of the following reasons: they lead to the experience of a great deal of psychic pain and discomfort; they motivate one to engage in self-defeating behaviour; they prevent one from carrying out behaviour necessary to reach one's goals; and they are associated with thinking that is skewed and distorted. Conversely, healthy negative emotions are healthy for any one or more of the following reasons: they alert one that one's goals are being blocked but do not immobilise one; they motivate one to engage in self-enhancing behaviour; they encourage the successful execution of behaviour necessary to reach one's goals; and they are associated with thinking that is balanced and realistic.

Three Basic Musts

While your clients will often express their irrational beliefs in personally distinctive terms, you might find it helpful to consider these individualistic beliefs to be variations of three 'basic musts'.

Basic Must No. 1: Demands about Self   The first basic must concerns your clients' demands about themselves and is often stated in these terms: '*I* must do well and be approved by significant others and if I'm not, then it is awful; I can't stand it, and I am a damnable person to some degree when I am not loved or when I do not do well.' These beliefs often lead to anxiety, depression, shame and guilt.

Basic Must No. 2: Demands about Others   The second basic must concerns your clients' demands about other people, and is often expressed as follows: '*You* must treat me well and justly, and it's awful and I can't bear it when you don't. *You* are damnable when you don't treat me well and you deserve to be punished for doing what you must not do.' Such beliefs are often associated with feelings of unhealthy anger, rage, passive-aggressiveness, and acts of violence.

Basic Must No. 3: Demands about the World/Life Conditions   The third basic must concerns your clients' demands about the world or *life conditions* and often takes the following form: 'Life conditions under which I live absolutely must be the way I want them to be and if they are not, it's terrible, I can't stand it, poor me.' This belief is associated with feelings of self-pity and hurt, and problems of self-discipline – for example, procrastination and addictive behaviour.

The Disturbance Matrix

It is possible to take the three basic musts and the two fundamental human disturbances to form a 3×2 disturbance matrix (see Figure 1.1).

	Ego disturbance	Discomfort disturbance
I must	A	B
You must	C	D
Life conditions must	E	F

Figure 1.1   *The disturbance matrix*

A   *Ego Disturbance – Demands about Self*   In this type of disturbance, it is quite clear that the person concerned is making demands about himself and the issue concerns his attitude towards himself. Thus, the major derivative from the demand concerns some variation of self-depreciation: for example, 'I must obtain a good degree and if I don't I am no good.'

B *Discomfort Disturbance – Demands about Self* Here, the person makes demands about himself but the real issue concerns his attitude towards discomfort: for example, 'I must obtain a good degree because if I don't, life conditions will be harsh and I couldn't bear that.'

C *Ego Disturbance – Demands about Others* Here, the person makes demands about another person, but the real issue concerns his attitude towards himself. A common example of this is found when another person's behaviour serves as a threat to the person's self-esteem and his unhealthy anger about the other's behaviour serves to protect his self-esteem: for example, 'You must treat me nicely because if you do not then that proves that I am no good.'

D *Discomfort Disturbance – Demands about Others* Here, the person makes demands about others but the real issue concerns the realm of discomfort: for example, 'You must treat me nicely because I couldn't stand life conditions if you do not.'

E *Ego Disturbance – Demands about Life Conditions* Here, on the surface, the person makes demands about some aspect of life conditions, but the real issue concerns his attitude towards himself: for example, 'Life conditions must be easy for me because if they are not then that's just proof of my worthlessness.'

F *Discomfort Disturbance – Demands about Life Conditions* This kind of disturbance is a more impersonal form of low frustration tolerance. It is often seen when a person loses his temper with inanimate objects: for example, 'My car absolutely must not break down because I couldn't stand the frustration if it did.'

Distinction between Healthy and Unhealthy Negative Emotions

We earlier made a distinction between healthy and unhealthy negative emotions (see p. 8). In this context it is important to realise that people can hold elements of rational and irrational beliefs at the same time, and they can easily transform what are called their partial desires into demands. Thus, I may hold the partial rational belief: 'I want to get a good degree' and then transform it into an irrational belief: 'Since I want to get a good degree, I must achieve one.' Consequently, it is important for counsellors to discriminate between their clients' full rational and irrational beliefs. A full preference[1], for example, asserts the person's desire and negates his must as in the belief: 'I want to get a good degree, but I don't have to get one.' When such distinctions are made it is easier to distinguish between healthy and unhealthy negative emotions. To reiterate the point made on p. 8 healthy negative emotions are associated with rational beliefs and unhealthy negative emotions with irrational beliefs.

We will now consider the distinction between healthy and unhealthy negative emotions in greater detail. In the emotions that follow the healthy negative emotion is listed first.

Concern vs. Anxiety   Concern is an emotion that is associated with the belief, 'I hope that this threat does not happen, but there is no reason why it must not happen. If it does it would be unfortunate, but not terrible.' Anxiety, on the other hand, occurs when the person believes, 'This threat must not happen and it would be awful if it did.'

Sadness vs. Depression   Sadness is deemed to occur when the person believes, 'It is very unfortunate that I have experienced this loss, but there is no reason why it should not have happened. It is bad that it happened, but not terrible.' Depression, on the other hand, is associated with the belief, 'This loss absolutely should not have occurred and it is terrible that it did.' Here, when the person considers herself responsible for the loss, she will tend to depreciate herself: '*I* am no good', whereas if the loss is outside the person's control he or she will tend to damn the world/life conditions: '*It* is terrible.' REBC theory holds that it is the philosophy of demandingness implicit in such evaluations that leads the person to consider that he or she will never get what he or she wants, an inference that is associated with feelings of hopelessness. Thus, for example: 'Because I must always get the things I really want and did not get it this time, I'll never get it at all. It's hopeless!'

Remorse vs. Guilt   Feelings of remorse occur when a person acknowledges that he has broken his moral code, for example, but accepts himself as a fallible human being for doing so. The person feels badly about the act or deed but not about himself because he holds the belief, 'I prefer not to act badly, but I am not immune from doing so. If I do, it's bad but I can accept myself as a fallible human being who has done the wrong thing.' Guilt occurs when the person condemns himself as bad, wicked, or rotten for acting badly. Here, the person feels badly both about the act and his 'self' because he holds the belief: 'I must not act badly and if I do it's *awful* and I am a *rotten* person!'

Disappointment vs. Shame   Feelings of disappointment occur when a person acts 'stupidly' in public, for example, acknowledges the stupid act, but accepts herself in the process. The person feels disappointed about her action but not with herself because she prefers, but does not demand, that she act well. Shame occurs when the person again recognises that she has acted 'stupidly' in public and then condemns herself for acting in a way that she absolutely should not have done. People who experience shame often predict that the watching audience will think badly of them, in which case they tend to agree with these perceived judgements. Thus, they often believe that they absolutely need the approval of these others.

Healthy Anger vs. Unhealthy Anger Healthy anger occurs when another person disregards an individual's rule of living, for example. The person who is healthily angry does not like what the other has done, but does not depreciate him or her for doing it. Such a person tends to believe, 'I wish the other person had not done that and I don't like what he/she did, but it does not follow that he/she must not break my rule.' In unhealthy anger, however, the person does believe that the other absolutely must not break the rule and thus depreciates the other for doing so.

Table 1 gives an extended list of the major emotional problems for which clients seek counselling and their constructive alternatives. It presents both the type of belief and the inferences most commonly associated with each of the emotions listed in the table.

Acquisition and Perpetuation of Psychological Disturbance

Rational emotive behavioural theory does not put forward an elaborate account of the way in which we as humans acquire psychological disturbance. This is because of the view discussed earlier that we have a biological tendency to think irrationally. However, rational emotive behavioural theory does acknowledge that environmental variables do contribute (and sometimes greatly) to our tendency to make ourselves disturbed by our irrational beliefs. Thus, if I have been treated harshly by my parents I am more likely to make demands about myself and about uncomfortable life conditions than I would be if my parents had treated me well. However, this is not always the case and we have met people who have had a harsh upbringing, but have made fewer demands on themselves, others, and life conditions than do some of my clients who have had a much more favourable upbringing. Thus, rational emotive behavioural theory stresses that humans vary in their disturbability. The REBC view of the acquisition

Table 1   *Healthy and unhealthy negative emotions and their cognitive correlates*

Major inferences[1] related to personal domain[2]	Type of belief	Emotion	Healthiness of emotion
Threat or danger	Irrational	Anxiety	Unhealthy
Threat or danger	Rational	Concern	Healthy
Loss (with implications for future); failure	Irrational	Depression	Unhealthy
Loss (with implications for future); failure	Rational	Sadness	Healthy
Breaking of personal rule (other or self); other threatens self; frustration	Irrational	Unhealthy (or damning) anger	Unhealthy
Breaking of personal rule (other or self); other threatens self; frustration	Rational	Healthy (or non-damning) anger	Healthy
Breaking of own moral code; failing to live up to own moral code; hurting someone's feelings	Irrational	Guilt	Unhealthy
Breaking of own moral code; failing to live up to own moral code; hurting someone's feelings	Rational	Remorse	Healthy
Other betrays or lets down self (self non-deserving)	Irrational	Hurt	Unhealthy
Other betrays or lets down self (self non-deserving)	Rational	Sorrow	Healthy
Threat to a significant relationship posed by another	Irrational	Unhealthy jealousy	Unhealthy
Threat to a significant relationship posed by another	Rational	Healthy jealousy	Healthy
Personal weakness revealed publicly – others' judgement of self negative; personal weakness revealed to self with others' negative judgement of self in mind	Irrational	Shame	Unhealthy
Personal weakness revealed publicly – others' judgement of self negative; personal weakness revealed to self with others' negative judgement of self in mind	Rational	Disappointment	Healthy
Other has something of value not possessed by self	Irrational	Unhealthy envy	Unhealthy
Other has something of value not possessed by self	Rational	Healthy envy	Healthy

1 Inference = An interpretation which goes beyond observable reality but which gives meaning to it; may be accurate or inaccurate.
2 The objects – tangible and intangible – in which a person has an involvement constitute a person's personal domain (Beck, 1976). Rational emotive behavioural theory distinguishes between ego and comfort aspects of the personal domain although these aspects frequently interact.

of psychological disturbance can be encapsulated in the view that we as humans are not made disturbed simply by our experiences; rather we bring our ability to disturb ourselves to these experiences.

Rational emotive behavioural theory does, however, put forward a more elaborate account of how we perpetuate our psychological disturbance. First, it argues that we do so because we lack three major insights: (a) psychological disturbance is primarily determined by rigid and extreme irrational beliefs that we hold about ourselves, others, and the world; (b) we remain disturbed by re-indoctrinating ourselves in the present with these irrational beliefs; and (c) the only long-term way of overcoming psychological disturbance is to work against our irrational beliefs and against our tendency to think irrationally and act dysfunctionally.

Secondly, rational emotive behavioural theory holds that we perpetuate our disturbances though our actions and subsequent modes of thought. You will recall that C in the REBC model stands for 'consequence'. When a person thinks irrationally at B about an activating event at A, then I have shown that that person will experience an unhealthy negative emotion at C. But, the person will also tend to act self-defeatingly at C (behavioural consequence) and think unrealistically at C (cognitive consequence). These behaviours and subsequent modes of thought frequently serve to strengthen the person's conviction in his irrational beliefs at B and in doing so they serve to perpetuate the person's psychological disturbance.

So far we have concentrated on behaviours and cognitions that help to maintain the person's psychological problems once the person's irrational beliefs and associated unhealthy negative emotions have been fully activated. In addition, as humans we also have the ability to act and think in ways that prevent our irrational beliefs (and associated unhealthy negative emotions) from being activated. However, we act and think in these ways because of the existence of our irrational beliefs which exert an influence on our behaviour and thinking even though they are latent. When we act and think in ways that serve to prevent the full activation of our irrational beliefs we are still perpetuating these beliefs and the psychological problems that these beliefs lead to. We will not focus on this issue here because it is an advanced issue and requires more space than we can give it in this introductory text (see Dryden, 1999, for a fuller discussion of this topic).

Thirdly, REBC theory contends that we perpetuate our psychological problems because we adhere to a philosophy of low frustration tolerance

(LFT). Thus, we tend to be short-range hedonists and to believe that we cannot stand discomfort. Even when we realise that we disturb ourselves with our beliefs in the present, we tend to think that this awareness alone will lead us to overcome our problems. Clients who have LFT beliefs will do poorly in rational emotive behavioural counselling and other forms of counselling as well because they steadfastly refuse to make themselves uncomfortable in the present so that they can become comfortable later. In particular, they tend to procrastinate about putting into practice outside counselling sessions what they have learnt inside counselling sessions and will frequently make a variety of 'good excuses' as to why they failed to do their homework assignments.

A fourth major way in which we perpetuate our psychological disturbances is explained by the fact that we often make ourselves disturbed (meta-disturbances) about our original disturbances. Thus, clients often make themselves anxious about their anxiety, guilty about their unhealthy anger, depressed about their depression, ashamed about feeling hurt, and so on. Unless clients tackle their meta-emotional problems before their original problems, when the presence of the former interferes with the work that they need to do on the latter, they will quite often impede themselves from overcoming these original disturbances. Thus, if a person condemns himself for his anger problem, he will get caught up in his self-blaming depression which will, in itself, tend to stop him from dealing with his original anger problem.

Fifthly, rational emotive behavioural counsellors agree with their psychoanalytic colleagues that we frequently employ defences to ward off threats to our ego and to our level of comfort. Using such defensive manoeuvres means that we can refrain from taking personal responsibility for our problems when they exist, preferring to blame others or life conditions for our problems. When this happens in counselling, such clients tend to resist the basic message of the rational emotive behavioural approach, namely that they *make themselves* disturbed, because if they were to accept this responsibility then they would, for example, severely condemn themselves. Unless the ideas that underlie their defensiveness are uncovered and dealt with, then little progress is possible.

Sixthly, we often perpetuate our problems because we get some kind of payoff from having these problems. Thus, we may get a lot of attention from others for having psychological problems which we are loath to do without, or our problems may protect us in our minds from having more severe problems. When a person receives some kind of payoff from having a psychological problem, such as attention from others, she is reluctant to work to overcome her problem because she may fear that she might lose the attention from others which she demands. When the psychological problem protects the person in her own mind from a more severe psychological problem then she will not be motivated to give up the existing emotional problem unless she can also be helped to deal with the problem that she fears she might encounter.

Finally, we often perpetuate our own problems because we make self-fulfilling prophecies. Thus, a man who has difficulties in trusting women may, when he meets a new woman, be quite suspicious of her and indirectly discourage her from having warm intimate feelings towards him. This may lead to her leaving him which would confirm in his mind his original idea that women were not to be trusted. Unless clients who make self-fulfilling prophecies are encouraged to see the contribution that they make to these prophecies, they are likely to persist in perpetuating their problems.

Theory of Therapeutic Change

The rational emotive behavioural theory of therapeutic change is basically a simple one. It states that if clients are to overcome their emotional and behavioural problems, they need to: (a) acknowledge that they have a problem; (b) identify and overcome any meta-disturbances about this problem; (c) identify the irrational belief that underpins the original problem; (d) understand why their irrational belief is, in fact, irrational (that is, illogical, inconsistent with reality, and will give them poor results in life); (e) realise why the rational alternative to this irrational belief is logical, consistent with reality, and will give them better results; (f) challenge their irrational belief so that they begin to strengthen their conviction in the rational alternative; (g) use a variety of cognitive, emotive, imaginal and behavioural assignments to strengthen their conviction in their rational belief and weaken their conviction in their irrational belief; (h) identify and overcome obstacles to therapeutic change using the same sequence as above while accepting themselves for their tendency to construct such obstacles; and (i) keep working against their tendency to think and act irrationally.

Key Elements in Rational Emotive Behavioural Practice

The Goals of Rational Emotive Behavioural Counselling

Rational emotive behavioural counselling is a system of counselling which is designed to help people to minimise their emotional disturbances and self-defeating behaviour and to encourage them to live a more meaningful and happier existence. In doing so, rational emotive behavioural counsellors help their clients to consider ways in which they prevent themselves from actualising themselves, by focusing on the irrational beliefs that underpin their emotional and behavioural problems. REB counsellors, then, encourage their clients: (a) to think more rationally (logically, flexibly, and scientifically); (b) to feel more healthily; and (c) to act more efficiently in order to achieve their basic goals and purposes.

A standard goal is to encourage clients to identify their original and meta-emotional and behavioural problems and to overcome these. However, a more ideal goal – and one that not all clients attain – is to encourage clients to make a profound philosophic change, meaning that they will: (a) give up making demands on themselves, others, and the world; (b) refrain from making extreme ratings of themselves, others, and the world; (c) accept themselves and other people as fallible human beings; (d) accept the world as being too complex to merit a global rating; and (e) tolerate discomfort when it is in their best interests to do so. Thus, rational emotive behavioural counsellors encourage their clients to get over the emotional and behavioural problems for which they seek counselling in the first place and wherever possible encourage them to minimise their tendency to disturb and to defeat themselves.

While rational emotive behavioural counsellors pursue this ideal goal of encouraging clients to make a profound philosophic change whenever possible, they acknowledge that their clients may not be interested in making such a radical shift in their belief system and they also recognise that many clients may not be able to embark on such a radical project. Thus, while REB counsellors offer their clients an opportunity to embark on a more radical restructuring of their belief system, they are flexible in adjusting their goals to meet their clients' goals.

This flexibility is also shown in the work of rational emotive behavioural counsellors with clients who are either unable or unwilling to work towards developing a new rational philosophy about specific elements of their lives. In such cases, REB counsellors will modify their therapeutic goals and encourage their clients to: (a) make changes in their inferences; (b) change the negative events in their lives; and (c) modify their behaviour so that they get some immediate benefit from the counselling process. However, rational emotive behavioural counsellors do recognise that for the most part such clients are vulnerable to future disturbance because they have not addressed the core of their emotional and behavioural problems – that is, the musturbatory and dogmatic demands that they make about themselves, others, and the world. Thus, rational emotive behavioural counsellors are willing to compromise and do not dogmatically insist that their clients always work towards addressing and overcoming their musturbatory beliefs (Dryden, 1996).

Whenever possible, however, REB counsellors strive to encourage their clients to internalise the three major REBC insights that were outlined on p. 14. To reiterate, this means helping clients to acknowledge: (a) that past or present activating events do not cause their disturbed emotional and behavioural consequences – rather it is their irrational beliefs about these activating events that largely create their disturbed feelings and behaviours; (b) that irrespective of how they have disturbed themselves in the past, they now upset themselves largely because they keep re-indoctrinating themselves in the present with their irrational beliefs; and (c) that although they are human and very easily, and to some degree naturally, tend to disturb themselves by clinging to their self-defeating thoughts, feelings, and actions, nevertheless they can largely (but not totally) overcome their disturbances in the long run. They can do this by working hard and repeatedly, both to dispute their irrational beliefs and to counteract the effects of these beliefs by strongly acting against them.

The Counselling Relationship

REBC does not dogmatically insist that one specific kind of counselling relationship be established between counsellor and client; indeed, rational emotive behavioural counsellors are encouraged to be flexible with respect to the kind of relationships they develop with different clients. Nevertheless it is true to say that rational emotive behavioural counsellors tend to favour establishing certain therapeutic conditions and therapeutic styles with their clients.

Therapeutic conditions   As has been discussed above, one of the most important goals that rational emotive behavioural counsellors have is to encourage their clients to accept themselves unconditionally as fallible human beings who often act self-defeatingly but who are never essentially good or bad. Given this stance, rational emotive behavioural counsellors themselves strive to accept their clients unconditionally and try not to denigrate their clients or dogmatically to insist that their clients must behave in certain ways, either within or outside counselling sessions. However, this does not prevent rational emotive behavioural counsellors from bringing to the attention of their clients aspects of their clients' behaviour which are self-defeating and impede the goals of other people. Ideally, then, a counselling relationship is established where both counsellor and client strive to accept self and other as fallible. The preferred REB counselling relationship, therefore, is an egalitarian one where both participants are equal in their humanity, although unequal at the outset with respect to expertise and skills in personal problem-solving.

Partly because of the egalitarian nature of the counselling relationship, rational emotive behavioural counsellors strive to be as open as therapeutically desirable and do not refrain from disclosing personal information about themselves should their clients ask for it, except when they judge that their clients would use such information either against themselves or against their counsellors. However, such openness has therapeutic purposes and is not disclosure for its own sake. Thus, when rational emotive behavioural counsellors disclose that they have in the past experienced problems similar to those of their clients, it is not only to indicate to clients that they are on an equal footing as humans with their clients, but also to teach their clients what they did to overcome these problems. In doing so, rational emotive behavioural counsellors serve as credible and encouraging role models. The basic message is: 'I am human too, I have experienced similar problems to you in the past, I overcame them and this is how I overcame them. Perhaps you can learn from my experience and take elements of it and apply this to your own problem-solving efforts.'

The world of counselling has been heavily influenced by the work of Carl Rogers (1957), and in particular his statements concerning the importance of certain core therapeutic conditions – that is, counsellor empathy, genuineness, and unconditional positive regard. Rational emotive behavioural counsellors would agree with these, particularly the importance of unconditional acceptance and genuineness. With respect to empathy, rational emotive behavioural counsellors offer their clients not only affective empathy – that is, communicating that they understand how their clients feel, but also philosophic empathy – that is, showing them that they also understand the philosophies that underpin these feelings.

The one disagreement rational emotive behavioural counsellors have with a large majority of counsellors from other therapeutic orientations concerns the role of counsellor warmth in the counselling process. Rational emotive behavioural counsellors argue that offering clients unconditional acceptance is more important than offering them counsellor warmth. In REBC the latter, particularly when this is excessive, has two major risks. First, counsellor warmth may unwittingly reinforce clients' dire need for love and approval – an irrational belief which is believed to lie at the core of much psychological disturbance. Secondly, counsellor warmth may also unwittingly reinforce the philosophy of low frustration tolerance that many clients have. This is particularly the case if being warm means refraining from actively encouraging, and in some cases strongly pushing clients to involve themselves in uncomfortable experiences for the long-term benefit of achieving therapeutic change.

Therapeutic Style   Ellis (1994) recommends that rational emotive behavioural counsellors adopt an active-directive therapeutic style with most clients. He argues that this style is important, particularly at the beginning of counselling in that it encourages clients to go quickly and efficiently to the philosophic core of their emotional and behavioural problems. However, effective rational emotive behavioural counsellors vary their therapeutic styles and can adopt a variety of styles to fit with the therapeutic requirements of different clients. Thus, for example, they would adopt: (a) a formal therapeutic style with clients who believe that effective counsellors should be businesslike and expert; (b) a more informal style with clients who value interacting with a friendly and more personally involved counsellor; and (c) a tough no-nonsense style with clients who seem to benefit from such a therapeutic style. In addition, there may be indications for adopting different therapeutic styles with clients who have different personality styles. Thus, Beutler (1983) has argued that it is important to avoid developing an overly friendly, emotionally charged style of interaction with 'histrionic' clients, an overly intellectual style with obsessive-compulsive clients, and an overly directive style with clients who very easily retreat into passivity. However, much more research is needed on this question of therapeutic flexibility with respect to counsellor style in REBC before any more definitive statements can be made on this issue.

Ellis (1987a) has often noted that emotional disturbance incorporates an attitude where the person takes life *too* seriously. Given that, rational emotive behavioural counsellors like to be appropriately humorous with their clients wherever possible. In doing so they demonstrate empathically and humorously to clients the comic aspects of their dogmatic irrational beliefs and teach their clients the therapeutic benefits of taking a serious but not overly serious attitude towards life. It is important to stress that this is done from a position of unconditional acceptance of clients and that when humorous interventions are employed, they are directed not at the clients themselves, but at their self-defeating thoughts, feelings, and actions. It should be noted, however, that some clients do not benefit from such humour and thus, again, the principle of therapeutic flexibility applies – vary your style of intervention to maximise your therapeutic relationships with different clients.

It is important to realise, as will be shown in Part 3, that the relationship between counsellor and client does change during the process of rational emotive behavioural counselling, particularly with respect to the active-directive aspects of the counsellor's style. Thus, when REBC is effective, the counsellor increasingly encourages the client to assume more responsibility for therapeutic change and, correspondingly, the counsellor's level of directiveness fades. When this occurs, rational emotive behavioural counsellors take a less directive prompting role, encouraging their clients to put into practice elements of the REBC problem-solving method which they have increasingly used during the early and middle stages of counselling.

Working Alliance   Another way of considering the REBC view of the therapeutic relationship is by employing Bordin's (1979) concept of the working alliance. He argued that there are three components of the alliance:

(a) the bond between counsellor and client. We have already discussed REBC's stance on these interpersonal features of the alliance;
(b) the goals of counsellor and client. In REBC, as we shall see, the counsellor helps the client to set specific, measurable and achievable goals and endeavours to stay focused on helping the client to work towards these goals;
(c) the tasks that counsellor and client need to execute to help the clients achieve his or her goals. In REBC, the counsellor is explicit about her own tasks and the tasks of her client. Once the client agrees to carry out his tasks, the REB counsellor helps him to do so, sometimes explicitly training him in important self-help skills. The important components of the task domain of the alliance are that the client can

see the relationship between him carrying out his tasks and achieving his goals; the tasks that he has agreed to carry out are potent enough to effect progress towards goal achievement; both parties understand and agree to carry out their own tasks, and have confidence that the other will execute their tasks, and the counsellor is proficient in carrying out her therapeutic tasks.

Emphasis on Examining Irrational Beliefs

We argued earlier that rational emotive behavioural theory adheres to the principle of psychological interactionism – namely, that beliefs, feelings, and behaviours cannot be separated from one another and in reality interact, often in quite complex ways. However, it is true that rational emotive behavioural counsellors direct much of their therapeutic attention to helping clients to examine their irrational beliefs, using cognitive, emotive, imaginal, and behavioural methods. This emphasis on examining irrational beliefs involves the skills of: (a) detecting the presence of such irrational beliefs; (b) discriminating them from rational beliefs; and (c) engaging in a questioning process, whereby clients are encouraged to question how logical, consistent with reality, and pragmatic their irrational beliefs are. However, it should be noted once again that although examining irrational beliefs is a central component to rational emotive behavioural counselling (DiGiuseppe, 1991), it is by no means the only defining feature of this approach to counselling. We wish to underscore this because many critics, and indeed many researchers who have carried out empirical studies on REBC, seem to equate it with its cognitive-restructuring aspects. Thus, while a central core of REBC does involve helping clients to examine their irrational beliefs and to replace these with rational beliefs, this is done in many different ways, as will be shown below.

Multimodal Emphasis

Rational emotive behavioural counsellors agree with Arnold Lazarus (1981) that it is important to take a multimodal approach to counselling. Thus, rational emotive behavioural counsellors encourage their clients to use many cognitive, emotive-evocative, imaginal, and behavioural techniques in the pursuit of changing their irrational ideas. In addition, because REBC stresses the biological as well as the environmental and social sources of human disturbance, rational emotive behavioural counsellors favour both the use of medication where appropriate, and of physical techniques (including nutrition, exercise, and relaxation methods) as an adjunct to the therapeutic process. However, such methods are used to encourage clients to work towards changing their irrational philosophies and are not used necessarily as an end in themselves.

Selective Eclecticism

Rational emotive behavioural counselling is what I (WD) have called a theoretically consistent approach to eclecticism (Dryden, 1987). This means that rational emotive behavioural counsellors are encouraged to use a wide range of therapeutic techniques originated by counsellors from other therapeutic schools. However, in doing so they would not accept the theoretical principles advocated by these other theorists; rather, techniques are freely borrowed from other schools with the major purpose of encouraging clients to identify, challenge, and change their irrational beliefs. As such, REBC de-emphasises the use of methods which discourage or impede clients from adopting a direct focus on changing their irrational ideologies. Thus, it avoids, although not in any absolute sense, using procedures that: (a) help people become more dependent – for example, the creation of a transference neurosis and the use of therapist as a strong reinforcer; (b) encourage clients to become more gullible and suggestible – for example, certain kinds of Pollyanna-ish positive-thinking methods; (c) are long-winded and inefficient – for example, free association and other psychoanalytic methods that discourage clients from focusing on their irrational beliefs; (d) help people to feel better in the short term rather than to get better in the long term – for example, some experiential techniques such as getting in touch with and fully expressing one's feelings; (e) have dubious validity and have not received empirical support from research studies even though proponents claim great therapeutic success for these procedures – for example, neurolinguistic programming; (f) include anti-scientific and mystical philosophies – for example, faith healing and astrology; and (g) appear to be harmful to a variety of clients – for example, encouraging clients, as in primal therapy, to scream, shout, and to express their angry feelings in an explosive manner.

It should be noted, however, that REB counsellors may use some of the above techniques for specific purposes. Thus, for example, experiential techniques can be used to help people to identify emotions prior to encouraging them to identify the irrational beliefs that underpin these emotions. Counsellor warmth may be warranted when clients are severely depressed; here the fact that the counsellor may show that he or she is very caring and concerned may inspire hope in such clients. In addition, Ellis (2002) has argued that he may be prepared to use some of these inefficient techniques with clients as a last resort when all else has failed.

The Importance of Homework

Most rational emotive behavioural counsellors see their clients for one hour a week. This means that for the remaining 167 hours in the week, their clients are on their own. This is a salutary reminder to those who claim that what goes on within counselling sessions has more therapeutic impact than what goes on between counselling sessions. Ellis has argued from REBC's inception that clients who put into practice between sessions what they have learned within sessions will gain more from counselling than clients who steadfastly refuse to act on what they have learned in counselling sessions. Thus, for rational emotive behavioural counsellors, encouraging clients to execute properly negotiated and well-designed homework assignments is considered to be a central part of the counselling process. Indeed, Ellis (1983a) and Persons et al. (1988) have reported empirical data to suggest that clients who carry out homework assignments in cognitively oriented approaches to counselling achieve a better outcome than clients who do not execute such assignments. Therefore effective rational emotive behavioural counsellors pay a lot of attention to the concept of homework in counselling, devoting sufficient time to discussing why this is a central part of the counselling process and to negotiating such assignments with their clients. In particular, they pay specific attention to factors which may discourage clients from successfully carrying out homework assignments and attempt to trouble-shoot such obstacles to psychotherapeutic change.

Confronting and Overcoming Obstacles to Change

We mentioned directly above that an important aspect of rational emotive behavioural counselling concerns identifying and overcoming obstacles to therapeutic change that arise when clients attempt to execute homework assignments. However, obstacles to change pervade the entire counselling process, and, given this clinical fact, rational emotive behavioural counsellors attempt to engage their clients in a co-operative exploration concerning the nature of these obstacles. If the obstacles to change can be attributed to the clients, counsellors will first identify the irrational beliefs that underpin their resistant behaviour. This having been done, counsellors urge their clients to overcome these obstacles so that they do not unduly interfere with the nature of therapeutic change.

Obstacles to change can occur: (a) within the counselling relationship; (b) within the client; and (c) within the counsellor. When obstacles to change occur within the counselling relationship it may be that the particular match between counsellor and client is not a good one. The best way of handling this may be a judicious referral to a different rational emotive behavioural counsellor. In addition, it has to be acknowledged that some clients do not find rational emotive behavioural counselling a helpful therapeutic method and may well do better with a different approach to counselling. This is because the ideas central to REBC – namely, that one's emotional disturbance is determined by one's presently held irrational beliefs and that one has to work and practise to overcome one's emotional and behavioural problems – are at variance with the viewpoint of the client and no amount of counsellor intervention may change the client's mind on these points. Here, a judicious referral to a counsellor from a different school may be indicated.

However, relationship obstacles to change can occur because the counsellor has unwittingly adopted a therapeutic style which is implicitly reinforcing the client's difficulties. Thus, the counsellor may offer the client too much warmth and inadvertently reinforce the client's need for approval, or the counsellor may adopt an overly directive style of interaction which encourages an already passive client to become more passive both in the counselling situation and in everyday life. It is important for counsellors to monitor their style of participation and to ask themselves continually whether their therapeutic style is encouraging or discouraging their clients from changing.

The second source of obstacles to therapeutic change resides in clients themselves, an issue which will be discussed further in Part 3. However, it should be noted here that clients may have irrational beliefs about certain aspects of the REBC process which may discourage them from changing. In particular, they may well have a philosophy of low frustration tolerance towards taking major responsibility for effecting their own improvement. Thus, they may believe that they should not be expected to work hard in counselling and that doing so is too difficult and too uncomfortable. It is important that counsellors encourage their clients to identify, challenge, and change such impeding philosophies if the latter are to benefit from rational emotive behavioural counselling in the long term.

Rational emotive behavioural counsellors are by no means immune from their own self-defeating beliefs, which may well serve as obstacles to the change process. Ellis (1983b) has outlined five major counsellor irrational beliefs that may serve as obstacles to client change:

1   I have to be successful with all of my clients practically all of the time.
2   I must be an outstanding counsellor, clearly better than other counsellors that I know or hear about.
3   I have to be greatly respected and loved by all my clients.
4   Since I am doing my best and working so hard as a counsellor, my clients must be equally hard-working and responsible, must listen to me carefully, and must always push themselves to change.
5   Because I'm a person in my own right, I must be able to enjoy myself during counselling sessions and to use these sessions to solve my personal problems as much as to help clients with their difficulties.

The presence of these beliefs may lead counsellors to back off from strongly encouraging their clients to change when this is called for, or to become inappropriately involved with their clients in a manner that sidetracks rational emotive behavioural counselling from its problem-solving focus. It is thus important for rational emotive behavioural counsellors to monitor their work regularly, to be prepared to accept themselves fully when they discover that they are sidetracking the counselling process inappropriately, and, when this is the case, to identify, challenge, and change the irrational beliefs that have produced the sidetracks. It is also important for counsellors to seek supervision of their work, since it may be that supervisors may be able to spot additional instances which may indicate that counsellors' own irrational beliefs have come to the fore and are serving as an obstacle to client change.

Force and Energy in Therapeutic Change

The theory of REBC holds that when clients are emotionally disturbed they tend to cling very forcefully and energetically to their main irrational beliefs, and that even when they have 'insight' into these beliefs they may still strongly believe them and refuse to give them up. In such circumstances, rational emotive behavioural counsellors are not loath to engage their clients in a very forceful and energetic process of examining their irrational beliefs and to encourage them to intervene very forcefully, vividly and energetically when they are examining their own irrational beliefs (Ellis, 1979). Thus, force and energy can be brought to the entire range of cognitive, imaginal, and behavioural assignments. This latter point serves to remind critics that rational emotive behavioural counselling does stress the emotive aspects of counselling and does bring passion to the counselling process. Without this focus on force and energy, clients will tend to challenge their irrational beliefs weakly and insipidly, and will thus experience very little benefit from the REBC process.

Characteristics of Effective Rational Emotive Behavioural Counsellors

In our long experience as trainers in REBC, we have noticed that effective rational emotive behavioural counsellors demonstrate the following qualities:

1   They are vitally interested in helping their clients.
2   They demonstrate an unconditional acceptance of their clients as fallible human beings but are not loath to confront their clients with their self-defeating behaviour.
3   They use a wide range of therapeutic techniques spawned from other schools but do so in a way consistent with the clinical theory of rational emotive behavioural counselling.
4   They demonstrate high frustration tolerance when clients do not change as quickly as they would like, adopt a problem-solving focus throughout counselling and do not use the counselling process for their own personal indulgence or to meet their own neurotic needs; in this regard they are neither under-involved nor over-involved with their clients.

Ellis (1987b) has argued that effective rational emotive behavioural counsellors have the additional following characteristics: (a) they enjoy being active and directive; (b) they are devoted to philosophy, science, logic, and empiricism; (c) they are skilled teachers and communicators; (d) they unconditionally accept themselves for their therapeutic errors, and work towards minimising these errors in the future; (e) they enjoy problem-solving; (f) they are experimental and take appropriate risks in the counselling process; (g) they have a good sense of humour which they use appropriately in counselling; (h) they are energetic and forceful; and (i) they apply rational emotive behavioural counselling in a way that is consistent with its clinical theory but in a flexible and non-dogmatic manner.

In this first part of the book we have outlined the basic principles of rational emotive behavioural counselling. In particular, we have discussed the theory that underpins its practice and have discussed the key elements of this approach to counselling in action. In Part 2, we will outline the rational emotive behavioural counselling sequence, and in the final part we will consider the process of REBC from beginning to end.

Note

1   A full-preference is sometimes known as a non-dogmatic preference.

Part 2

THE RATIONAL EMOTIVE BEHAVIOURAL COUNSELLING SEQUENCE

In this part, we will first give a brief overview of the rational emotive behavioural counselling sequence. The REB counselling sequence comprises six steps devoted to addressing clients' emotional disturbance and is outlined in Figure 2.1. The ABCDE model used by REB counsellors to understand and ameliorate this disturbance is outlined in Figure 2.2. The counselling sequence and the ABCDE model will be considered together to illustrate the application of REBC to an actual client problem. Secondly, we will introduce our client, Paula, to provide this illustration in step 1.

Throughout this part of the book we shall address you, the reader, directly and shall assume that you are dealing with your client's emotional problems one at a time. Thus, in specifying the rational emotive behavioural counselling sequence we will assume that you are working with a given client problem.[1]

An Overview of the Rational Emotive Behavioural Counselling Sequence

In this section, we will provide a brief overview of the counselling sequence and show how it is linked to the ABCDE model. We will consider each step separately and in detail throughout the rest of Part 2.

As will be discussed in Part 3, the initial stage of REB counselling often involves, first, greeting your client,[2] secondly, helping her to express her concerns and, thirdly, discussing her expectations for counselling and agreeing basic practicalities (e.g. fees, frequency and length of sessions). After you have done this, we suggest that you adopt a problem-solving attitude at the outset, and ask your client to select a problem for examination. If your client has more than one problem, a problem list can be drawn up and she can choose which problem to focus on first. Whichever problem is chosen, you will need to assess if it is connected to a meta-emotional problem, that is, an emotional problem about an emotional problem, such as shame at feeling anxious, or guilt about feeling angry. If there is a meta-emotional problem and it significantly interferes with work on the primary problem, it is usually desirable to work on this problem first (with your client's agreement). The meta-emotional problem, like the primary problem, is assessed within the ABC framework.

---

1   Selecting and investigating a problem.
2   Goal-setting.
3   Teaching the B–C connection and assessing irrational beliefs.
4   Examining irrational and rational beliefs.
5   Negotiating and reviewing homework assignments.
6   Working through.

Figure 2.1   *The rational emotive behavioural counselling sequence*

Situational A = client's objective description of the situation.

Critical A = client's subjective account of the most upsetting aspect of the situation.

iBs = irrational beliefs triggered by the critical A.

C = consequences – disturbed emotions, counterproductive behaviours and distorted thinking largely determined by holding iBs.*

D = disputing or examining iBs to moderate consequences at C.

E = new and effective (rational) outlook.

---

* We are only dealing with emotional and behavioural C's in this book. For the cognitive consequences of holding iBs, see Dryden (2002).

Figure 2.2   *REBC model for understanding and ameliorating emotional disturbance*

The problem selected for examination starts with the situational A, which is your client's objective account of the situation, and a disturbed emotion (e.g. guilt, anxiety, anger) is linked to this situation. Using the disturbed emotion (C) as a 'driving force' (e.g. 'What was anxiety-provoking in your mind about that situation?') usually uncovers a number of linked inferences, a procedure known as inference chaining. What your client is most upset about in this situation is called the critical A (i.e., the key inference has been located).

If your client presents you with a disturbed emotion when you ask for a problem (e.g. 'I feel so guilty'), you need to link this emotion to a situational A (e.g. 'In what specific situation do you feel guilty?') and then initiate the inference-chaining process to find the critical A. The critical A triggers the release or exposure of your client's irrational beliefs (B). Once the critical A has been found, your client can decide what would be a constructive goal in order to deal with her disturbed emotions in this situation.

The next step is to show your client that B, not A, largely determines C – this is known as teaching the B–C connection. Once this has been achieved, your client's irrational beliefs are disputed (D) or examined.[3] In essence, this process of examination seeks to show your client why her irrational beliefs are self-defeating and goal-blocking while her new rational beliefs are self-helping and goal-attaining (rational beliefs are examined in the same way as irrational beliefs). In order to attenuate her irrational beliefs and strengthen her rational beliefs, your client is encouraged to carry out agreed between-session assignments (homework) which are reviewed at the start of each session. Such assignments help your client to internalize a new or effective (E) rational outlook by translating knowledge (intellectual insight) into conviction (emotional insight). This process is known as working through. Once your client has made progress in managing one problem, she can select another one to focus on using the same counselling sequence. We will now discuss each step in greater detail.

Step 1: Selecting and Investigating a Problem

Once the introductions are over, the first order of REBC business is for you to ask your client what problem she would like to focus on. Such a rapid move into immediate problem discussion conveys a number of important messages your client. First, counselling time is precious and therefore you and your client need to 'get on with it' in tackling the latter's emotional problems. Second, it demonstrates that REBC is efficient, usually relatively brief, and highly focused in its problem-solving efforts – protracted counselling prolongs your client's suffering. Third, it signals to your client that you are going to be very active during the course of counselling and directive in keeping your client (and yourself) on track in ameliorating her problems.

However, it should not be forgotten that some clients will need more time to explore their problems – a less hurried atmosphere – and if you keep pushing your client for a definite problem to work on, it is likely to have an adverse impact on the development of a productive relationship (in these circumstances, the first homework task could be for your client to select a problem for examination). Here, as elsewhere in the counselling sequence, flexibility is the guiding principle of REBC.

Two Strategies for Problem Selection: Client Choice versus Client's Most Serious Problem

These two basic strategies can be used by you in attempting to elicit a problem from your client. The first strategy leaves the choice to your client while the second strategy is initiated by you: 'What are you presently most upset or troubled about in your life?' Either strategy usually yields client material for examination.

Meta-emotional Problems

One of the unique features of REBC is its focus on meta-emotional problems or what some REB counsellors refer to as secondary emotional problems (Ellis and Bernard, 1985). Meta-emotional problems are, literally, emotional problems about emotional problems such as being ashamed of feeling anxious, or being angry about feeling guilty, and can impede your client's progress (e.g. while you are focused on her primary problem of jealousy, her attention is on her angry feelings which are directed at her partner for 'forcing' her to seek help for her problem). You can check for the presence of meta-emotional problems with questions combined with illustrations: 'Are there any other issues or feelings that might prevent or distract you from discussing your panic attacks? What we mean by this is that some clients might feel angry or ashamed about having a problem in the first place as well as discussing it with a stranger such as myself. Does that ring any bells with you?' If a meta-emotional problem is detected, then the following three criteria can be used to determine if it should be examined first (Dryden et al., 2003):

1   If the meta-emotional problem interferes significantly with the work being done on your client's primary problem, e.g. she has frequent angry outbursts when discussing her depressed feelings about the end

of a relationship. Such interference can occur both in and out of the counselling session.

2   If, clinically speaking, the meta-emotional problem appears to be the more important of the two.

3   If she can see the sense of working on her meta-emotional problem first.

As noted above, clients who are reluctant to disclose an emotional problem may feel ashamed about having the problem or admitting it to you (shame is usually a key meta-emotional problem). You can attempt to surmount this difficulty by asking your client how she would feel if she did have an emotional problem about the situation under discussion, e.g. 'Just for argument's sake, how would you feel if you acknowledged that you are envious because your husband has a better-paid job than yours?' With clients who provide indications that they would feel ashamed, you can attempt to reach an agreement to work on shame first before encouraging disclosure of the original problem.

When Your Client Fails to Pinpoint a Problem Quickly

The 'problem' of not finding a problem can be handled by you in a number of ways. First, your client can be informed that she does not have to 'jump in at the deep end' by revealing straightaway her most painful problem (she might want to reveal it once she has 'road tested' the effectiveness of REBC on less troubling issues). A less threatening problem can be focused on by you suggesting to her that virtually everyone has some area in their life in which they are performing sub-optimally. This method can help to nudge some clients into a problem-solving focus.

Second, she can be encouraged to identify feelings and behaviours she wishes to increase (e.g. confidence) or decrease (e.g. anxiety) and attitudes she wants to change (e.g. the need to please everyone) or adopt (e.g. how to cope when the going gets tough). This approach can be particularly useful for clients who are largely unaware of what is involved in counselling or who are doubtful whether counselling can really help them. With these clients, it is particularly important for you to attend to induction procedures within REBC as a means of reducing client misunderstanding and eventual disillusionment with the counselling process (for a discussion of REBC induction procedures, see Dryden, 2002).

Third, a less direct way of helping your client to establish a problem area for intervention is by asking her what she would like to accomplish through counselling (e.g. being able to ask men out) and what is holding her back from achieving this goal (e.g. 'I always wait to be asked out which means I'm not asked out very often'). Such questioning can lead to a discussion of the self-defeating thoughts, feelings and behaviours that act as impediments to goal attainment (e.g. 'If I ask men out they'll probably say "no" because I'm not very attractive. Why should I put myself through that?').

Fourth, some clients, even though they have chosen to come for counselling, dislike the word 'problem' as it carries negative connotations for them (e.g. it is a sign of weakness, a loss of control in their lives). In these cases, you should use more client-friendly terms such as 'Are there any challenges in your life you would like to discuss?' or 'What concerns would you like to focus on?' The client can see herself as being in coaching rather than counselling, with you reconceptualising your role as a coach or consultant.

Obtain a Clear Description of the Problem and the Specific Context in which it Occurs

Clients frequently describe their problems in vague or confusing terms (e.g. 'It's something about commitment', or 'On one level it's about me not valuing me, on another level it's about me thinking too much about me, and yet on another level I feel I don't know me at all. You know what I mean?'). When this is the case with your client, encourage her to be clear and specific about the problem. For example, you can ask her what precisely is the 'something about commitment' and to whom or what? (Client's reply: 'The commitment is to move in with my boyfriend, but I worry about doing that.')

Such investigation helps you to begin to formulate your client's replies in terms of REBC's ABC model: the situational A is the possibility of moving in with her boyfriend and the emotional C is worry (the critical A, or what your client is most worried about if she moves in with her boyfriend, awaits discovery). Remember that a general problem is better understood through specific examples of its occurrence and that your client's level of emotional engagement with the problem is usually higher or more intense at the specific level than the general level (Neenan and Dryden, 2001).

Focus on a Disturbed Emotion at C

It is not emotions *per se* that are explored in REBC but disturbed emotions (e.g. anger, guilt, shame). A disturbed emotion – one that is prolonged rather than transient – is usually characterised by the emotional pain it inflicts upon your client, its contribution to her self-defeating behaviour and its role as an impediment to achieving her goals.

Part 1 of this book contained a compendium of feeling words used in REBC theory to distinguish between unhealthy (disturbed) and healthy (non-disturbed) negative emotions. It is highly unlikely that clients use these terms in the same way that REB counsellors do. Therefore, it is important for you and your client to agree on a shared vocabulary of emotional expression in order to reduce misunderstandings (Dryden, 1986). For example, you may accept without further exploration your client's description of herself as depressed following the end of a relationship; unfortunately, valuable therapy time is wasted on trying to help your client overcome her non-disturbed feelings of sadness (as it later emerges); in your client's mind, depression and sadness are synonymous.

A cognitive and behavioural profile of your client's 'depression' would have helped you to distinguish between the REBC view of sadness (e.g. still engaged in some way with the world – 'My life isn't over because the relationship ended') and depression (e.g. withdrawal from the world – 'I have no future since the relationship ended'). Whether the REBC emotional vocabulary is used or your client's idiosyncratic terms, it is important that both of you adhere to the agreed terminology.

Your client might describe her disturbed feelings in ways that are unclear to you such as 'stressed out', 'brassed off' or 'in bits'. It will be difficult for you to help your client ameliorate her disturbed feelings if she does not know which disturbed feelings are involved in her presenting problems. By helping your client to clarify her feelings in terms of REBC's unhealthy negative emotions, 'in bits' becomes 'deeply hurt'. If your client is unable to help you with this clarification process, analysing several situations where these disturbed feelings are experienced and/or listening for themes present in your client's thoughts can help you to pinpoint which disturbed feelings are involved. For example, after discussing several fraught situations at work, it is established that 'stressed out' primarily relates to anxiety and anger and the themes of betrayal and unfairness reveal that 'brassed off' refers to the blended emotion of angry hurt.

In Figure 2.2 we said that C in the ABCDE model represented emotional, behavioural and cognitive consequences. In practice, it is emotional C's rather behavioural ones that are investigated because REBC is primarily focused on emotional problem-solving. Behavioural C's often serve a protective or defensive function in helping clients to avoid experiencing disturbed feelings; e.g. procrastination allows a client to sidestep the intense discomfort of undertaking an onerous task; keeping quiet in a group helps another client to avoid realising her feared outcome of public humiliation if she says the wrong thing. When the maladaptive behaviour is dropped and your client either imagines carrying out the previously avoided activity or actually carries it out, the disturbed emotional C is usually quickly identified.

When discussing your client's disturbed feelings, it is very important that you use B–C language, that is, conveying to your client that she largely disturbs herself about adverse events in her life, for example 'How did you make yourself angry when your friend did not return the loan when he said he would?'; 'What are you anxious about when you think about asking a woman for a date?'; 'How did you make yourself depressed when you didn't get the promotion?' Conveying to the client that it is the situational A (the event) that causes C (emotion) – 'Not getting that promotion made you depressed' – undermines the principle and practice of emotional responsibility (i.e. that one's emotional disturbance is largely self-induced through rigid and extreme thinking). If your client does not accept emotional responsibility, it is highly unlikely that she will gain any significant or lasting benefit from REBC. Change begins when your client accepts responsibility for it (e.g. 'I make myself depressed because I keep on demanding that I absolutely should have got the promotion, but, as I didn't, I continue to see myself as a failure').

Locating the Critical A[4]

In assessing your client's problem, you are searching for the critical A, that is, the aspect of the situation which your client is most upset about and triggers her irrational belief (B) which, in turn, largely determines her emotional reaction at C (see Figure 2.2). A key technique for locating the critical A is inference chaining, that is, linking your client's personally significant inferences about the situation in order to pinpoint the triggering inference. Your client is asked a series of 'Let's assume . . . then what?' or variations on 'What does that mean to you?' questions in order to uncover the critical A. Inference chaining is greatly aided when you assume that each inference uncovered is temporarily true, even if they are all clearly distorted, in order to avoid premature disputing (irrational beliefs are the primary targets of disputing in REBC, not distorted inferences). In this example, the client is depressed (C) about failing to be selected for a job interview (situational A):

CLIENT: I have impressive qualifications, lots of experience. Why didn't they select me for an interview?
COUNSELLOR: What does it mean to you in not being selected?

[The counsellor sidesteps the 'Why?' question, as speculating on the motives of the company's decision is outside the remit of inference chaining. The therapist wants to pursue the personal implications for the client of the company's decision.]

CLIENT: They obviously can't think much of me despite all my achievements.
COUNSELLOR: Let's assume they don't think much of you despite all your achievements, then what?
CLIENT: [eyes moisten, voice drops, fists clench] Then no company will want me. I'll be unemployable.

[The intensity of the client's emotional, verbal and behavioural responses usually indicates that the critical A is near.]

COUNSELLOR: What does that mean to you or about you that you are unemployable?
CLIENT: No company will ever want me because I'm no good, washed-up, useless.
COUNSELLOR: Is that what you are most depressed about in not being selected for a job interview: that no company will ever want you because you are 'no good, washed-up, useless'? [Client nods his head repeatedly.]

[The critical A has been uncovered which includes self-depreciation beliefs – 'no good, washed-up, useless'.]

Avoid the following pitfalls when inference chaining:

- Pursuing theoretical inferences at the expense of personally meaningful ones, for example that ending up homeless or in prison could happen but these are not your client's actual worries. The pursuit of theoretical inferences occurs because you are on autopilot and assume that the critical A is always at the end of the inference chain (it can be anywhere in the chain). Also, you may forget to review the chain with your client in order to pinpoint emotional 'hot spots' in it or fail to pay attention to your client's emotional, behavioural and verbal clues that indicate whether she is moving towards the critical A or away from it.

- Becoming obsessive in the hunt for the critical A. This wastes valuable therapy time and can exhaust the patience of your client. This obsessiveness on your part is usually driven by your belief that 'I must find the critical A in order to prove I'm a competent therapist', and what may have begun as orderly detective work can end in an irritable inquisition: 'What are you most angry about in that situation then?' We would advise you, particularly if you are a trainee counsellor, to find a reasonably important or near-critical A to work on, make explicit the irrational beliefs embedded within this A and then show your client how to challenge these beliefs. This gets counselling moving, rather than becoming stalled through your obsessiveness (Neenan and Dryden, 2001). The critical A can be pinpointed later in counselling as more of your client's problem is revealed.

- Asking 'How do you feel about that?' questions instead of sticking to the emotion (e.g. guilt) that has been identified for investigation. Such questions may produce several emotions your client experiences in relation to the situation; however, they are not analysed in a batch but separately as each one has a discrete cognitive structure with its own critical A. If your client does report a new emotion emerging during inference chaining (e.g. initially hurt but now feeling angry) then she can decide which emotion will claim her attention for examination (other emotions can be examined later in counselling).

Paula

This client will be used throughout this section to illustrate the REBC sequence in action. Paula was a 30-year-old woman who worked as an interior designer. She had a successful career and a wide circle of friends. 'You would think that looking at me and my life that everything was fine', she said, 'but if you look closer you'll see me struggling.' She said she was struggling at work to manage an ever-increasing workload and was working long hours to 'keep on top of things'. She was reluctant to voice her concerns to her boss and feared that if the pressure at work was maintained much longer she might have a 'breakdown' (in discussing her presenting problem, no meta-emotional problems were revealed).

She said she felt trapped between relentless work pressures and her self-imposed ban on asking for help or requesting a slowdown in the amount of work passed to her ('I know it's the sensible thing to do to ask for help and sometimes I'm on the brink of doing it because I've had enough, but then I don't do it'). In order to establish an early problem focus as part of the socialisation process into REBC, I (MN) asked Paula for a specific example of when she was on the 'brink of doing it':

PAULA: I'm up to my eyeballs in work and he gave me another project to work on. Can't he see my situation? Do I have to fall apart at work before he gets the message? I get so angry at the injustice of it all. Then getting angry just gets me in more of a state than I already am.

[The client has not answered my question but has focused on the consequences for her of being given extra work.]

MICHAEL: OK, those are the continuing consequences of not asking for help. What we want to find out is how you hold yourself back from asking for help. Can you think of a specific example of when you were on the brink of asking for help but pulled back?

PAULA: Well, the other evening I was working late yet again and my boss was leaving the office and he joked before he left, 'Don't work too late now. All work and no pleasure as they say and you know what that leads to', and I thought to myself, 'If you know, why aren't you doing something about it?'

MICHAEL: But you were on the brink of asking for help, right?

PAULA: Yes, I was.

MICHAEL: We need to stay focused if we are going to discover what holds you back. Now let me write on the whiteboard 'Situational A: on the brink of asking your boss for help'. Now how do you feel as you think about asking for help.

PAULA: Relieved as I'm now going to start sorting things out.

MICHAEL: If you felt relieved why did you not ask him then?

PAULA: Well, I thought I was going to feel relieved, then I just felt overwhelmed and I couldn't do it.

MICHAEL: What emotion does 'overwhelmed' refer to?

PAULA: Anxiety, very anxious. I felt this panic beginning to grip me. I just couldn't get the words out. Like I was rooted to the spot.

MICHAEL: I'll write on the whiteboard 'C: emotional and behavioural consequences – very anxious/panicky and rooted to the spot'. Would it make sense to find out what lies behind your anxiety and panic, which, in turn, prevents you from asking your boss for help?

PAULA: Sounds like a good idea.

MICHAEL: OK. Now in order to find out what you are most anxious, panicky about in asking your boss for help, we need to go on an imaginary trip. I'm going to ask you a series of questions that will help us to sift through your thinking in this situation in order to discover what you are most anxious about, or, in REBC jargon, your critical A. OK?

PAULA: OK. I'm interested myself in finding this critical A, as you call it. I do need to get my head sorted out.

MICHAEL: Now, what's anxiety-provoking in your mind about asking your boss for help?

[The way I phrase the question emphasises that anxiety starts in the client's mind rather than generated by the situation.]

PAULA: Hmm. Well, what if he gets funny about it?

MICHAEL: Your reply is rather unclear: do you mean he will or won't get 'funny about it'?

[The client's reply is in the form of a question which I encourage her to answer in order to make the inference clearer.]

PAULA: He will get funny about it.

[The client's first inference.]

MICHAEL: Can I just clarify what you mean when you say 'he will get funny' about your request for help?

[Clarifying a client's remark is acceptable in inference chaining as long as the counsellor does not get absorbed into discussing it and thereby deflected from the search for the critical A.]

PAULA: He might think I'm not up to the job.

[Client's second inference.]

MICHAEL: And if he does think that, then what?
PAULA: Then he might wonder what's wrong with me.
MICHAEL: And what specifically is it that he might wonder is wrong with you?

[I want to be clear about the implied negative inference.]

PAULA: That I can't cope with the job.

[Client's third inference.]

MICHAEL: And if he does think that about you?
PAULA: I'd get angry.
MICHAEL: Why?

[I ask 'why?' to keep the client hunting for her critical A. If I ask questions such as 'What would you be angry about?', then new pathways could be opened up to find other critical A's but what the client is most anxious about in this situation may remain undiscovered. As a general rule, you can ask 'why?' questions when your clients provide you with emotional and behavioural consequences (C's) in reply to your enquiries about their inferences.]

PAULA: [*eyes moistening, voice dropping, staring at the floor*] Because he's looking down on me.

[The client's verbal, affective and behavioural responses indicate the critical A is close.]

MICHAEL: And if he is looking down on you?
PAULA: That would be dreadful.
MICHAEL: What would be dreadful about that?
PAULA: [*raising her head*] Who wants their boss to look down on them? Doesn't everyone want to do a good job and get ahead in life?

[The client is now making eye contact with me which she was not doing a few moments earlier. Some emotional heat has escaped from the inference chain, so to speak, and I need to retrace my steps to detect where the 'leak' occurred. I hypothesise that it occurred because I did not make explicit what the client thinks is behind her boss looking down on her and how this would lead to her conclusion 'That would be dreadful.']

MICHAEL: I'm sure many people would agree with that, but I would like to go back to something you said a moment ago. If your boss did look down on you, what do you think he would be thinking about you?

[I am asking the client to 'read' her boss's mind in order to discover what would be dreadful to her about his viewpoint.]

PAULA: [*staring at the floor again*] He would think I'm weak and inadequate for asking for help.
MICHAEL: And if he did think that, would you agree with him?

[I am trying to find out what is the more important aspect for her: his putative opinion of her or her agreement with it.]

PAULA: [quietly] Yes I would. I believe that asking for help is a sign of weakness. It shows you're inadequate.
MICHAEL: Is that what you're most anxious about in this situation: that you will reveal yourself as weak and inadequate if you ask your boss for help?

[I sum up what has been uncovered in order to check that the critical A has been located.]

PAULA: Yes. That's exactly it. I know it's silly but what can I do?

[The client's critical A has been revealed.]

Step 2: Goal-Setting

The best time to discuss goal-setting is when your client's critical A has been uncovered as it pinpoints what aspect of her problem is most troublesome or upsetting for her; this information then forms the basis for a specific goal to be agreed. Some issues in goal-setting will now be discussed.

Distinguishing Between Short-Term and Long-Term Goals

Your client may choose short-term goals because they involve less work and discomfort and bring immediate results. Such short-termism often perpetuates your client's problems rather than removes them (e.g. your client wants to learn distraction and relaxation techniques rather than actually face and overcome her panic disorder). Encourage your client to pursue goals that are more likely to endure through philosophical restructuring than if shored-up by quick fixes, that is, to remove rigid musts and absolute shoulds and their extreme derivatives and replace them with flexible and non-extreme alternatives (e.g. your client now enters those situations where she experiences panic attacks and forcefully reminds herself that she can stand the acute discomfort of the panic symptoms and that the attack will not last for more than three minutes if she stops scaring herself with catastrophic thoughts) (McKay et al., 1997).

Discourage Serenity in the Face of Adversity

This goal usually involves your client saying that she wants to feel, for example, 'calm', 'relaxed' or 'indifferent' about unpleasant life events. Such a goal often involves self-denial: why suppress her understandable desire that bad events should not occur? A possible reason for this suppression is that your client is unable to think rationally about such events and, therefore, she makes herself emotionally disturbed about them; hence her desire to feel calm or indifferent. You can suggest to her that there is a middle way between disturbance and denial: to accept the reality of events and then distinguish between what she can change and what she cannot.

For similar reasons, do not accept your client's goal that involves her feeling positive about adverse events (e.g. being mugged). Your client might try to convince herself that what happened to her was good because it is character building or because she can act as a sturdy role model for others such as her children. Again, your client is trying to persuade herself of something that she does not really believe or feel, and any positive feelings or noble forbearance she is trying to force herself to experience will probably be short-lived.

Help Your Client to State Her Goal in Positive Terms

This refers to clients stating what they want to do or feel rather than what they do not want to do or feel, e.g. 'I want to feel more confident in social situations' rather than 'I don't want to feel anxious in social situations'. As Cormier and Cormier observe:

> When the goal is stated positively, clients are more likely to encode and rehearse the things they want to be able to do rather than the things they want to avoid or stop. For example, it is fairly easy to generate an image of yourself watching TV. However, picturing yourself *not* watching TV is difficult. (1985: 223; emphasis in original)

When your client puts her goal in negative terms, you can help her to transform it into positive terms, for example, 'You say you don't want to get so angry when you're stuck in traffic jams, so how would you like to feel in those situations?'

Help Your Client to Translate Vague Goals into Specific Goals

Vague goals such as 'I want to be happy' are unhelpful because they do not indicate how such happiness is to be achieved. Translating your client's vague goals into specific ones begins when you ask such questions as 'What particular things would bring happiness into your life that are currently absent from it?' or 'What do you think you need to do in order to be happy?' Your client might say that she wants a partner, to lose weight and be fitter. The irrational beliefs hindering the achievement of these specific goals would be identified, challenged and changed.

When Your Client Sets Process Goals at the Expense of Outcome Goals

Some clients come to counselling to immerse themselves in extensive self-exploration rather than to set specific goals to work towards. REBC is outcome-focused, not process-focused, so if your client cannot shift her focus from endless introspection to acceptance of an agreed and clear treatment plan, then another form of counselling is indicated. However, other clients can be 'nudged' from process to outcome by such suggestions as, 'You say you want to understand why you got into this mess, but what goals would get you out of it? Working towards such goals not only pulls you out of the mess but also helps you to understand how you got into it.'

Guidelines for Goal-Setting (Neenan and Dryden, 2000)

A useful acronym to guide goal selection is SMART:

Simple and specific – 'I want to be relatively calm in the presence of spiders.'

Measurable – how will your client know she has achieved her goal?

Agreed – have you and your client agreed on the goal?

Realistic – is the goal within your client's control to achieve?

Timebound – can your client's goal be realised within the time she is prepared to spend in counselling?

Paula

Having discovered Paula's critical A through inference chaining in the previous dialogue (that she would reveal herself as weak and inadequate if she asked her boss for help), I now want to ascertain her goal for change.

PAULA: If you could help me in some way that I didn't need to ask for help, then I wouldn't have this problem.

MICHAEL: Let's say I could help you in that way, what belief would I be helping you to reinforce in your mind?

PAULA: I don't understand.

MICHAEL: I would be reinforcing or giving my approval to your idea that asking for help from your boss means you are weak and inadequate. I'm not prepared to agree to that goal. Also, if we could find a way by which you didn't need to ask for help, how long would it last for? Just this job or for the rest of your working life?

PAULA: OK, good point. I would have to ask for help at some point. I don't know what my goal is then.

MICHAEL: When we were looking at your problem you said, and I quote, 'I know it's the sensible thing to do to ask for help', so why not make that your goal?

PAULA: It would be a sensible goal but . . . I always end up in the same place about myself.

[Paula has doubts about this 'sensible goal' which need to be explored; if goal-setting is rushed, client and counsellor may be working towards an unsound or self-defeating goal.]

MICHAEL: But you could come to different conclusions about yourself when you ask for help, such as . . .?

[I am encouraging Paula to articulate a goal where she will 'end up in a new place about herself'.]

PAULA: That it's OK to ask for help.

[This seems to be the emergence of a positive, self-helping goal.]

MICHAEL: And how would you like to see yourself when you ask for help?

[I want to ascertain if she equates asking for help with a positive self-image. I am still probing for potential weaknesses in the stated goal.]

PAULA: Just as a normal person who needs help from time to time. Nothing more than that.

[This appears to be a rational belief in embryonic form that may aid goal-attainment. To what extent Paula's belief is rational will be examined in detail in Step 4.]

MICHAEL: And how might you feel with that view of yourself in mind?

[If Paula can really see herself as a 'normal person who needs help from time to time', then there should be a corresponding decrease in the level of emotional intensity she experiences when thinking about and/or asking for help.]

PAULA: Just feeling a bit queasy. That would be all right.
MICHAEL: What does 'a bit queasy' mean to you?

[I am probing to ascertain if 'a bit queasy' does reflect this decrease in emotional intensity.]

PAULA: Just a bit nervous, that's all. Can't expect to feel calm about it, can I?
MICHAEL: I'm just checking what it meant, so we are both referring to the same emotion when we use the term.
PAULA: (pondering) You know, this goal sounds good but can I achieve it?
MICHAEL: We'll come to that.

Step 3: Teaching the B–C Connection and Assessing Irrational Beliefs

My assessment of Paula's specific example of holding herself back from asking her boss for help looked like this when written on the whiteboard in my office:

Situational A = imagining asking her boss for help.

Critical A = 'I would reveal myself as weak and inadequate.'

B = (demand)? 'I am weak and inadequate' (conclusion).

[The irrational conclusion emerged during inference chaining. The possible presence of rigid demands in her thinking awaits assessment.]

C = very anxious/panicky and rooted to the spot.

Establishing the B–C connection is a crucial step in REBC assessment as it teaches your client the concept of emotional responsibility, that is, that emotional disturbance is largely self-induced through irrational thinking; it is not caused by events or others though these factors contribute, sometimes considerably, to your client's problems. In teaching the B–C connection, it is preferable for you to keep your story simple, clear and vivid as this is more likely to help your client grasp the significance of the story.

In our experience, those counsellors who opt for elaborate stories are apt to confuse themselves as well as their clients about the message they are attempting to communicate. Therefore, B–C can also stand for Brief–Clear in teaching emotional responsibility. You can choose a story that is related to your client's problem if it will make more of an impact on her, or one that is unrelated to it if she does not display sufficient detachment in listening to a story similar to her own. The best starting point is to ask your client for her preference:

PAULA: You can use my problem for the story.

MICHAEL: OK. Now it is not events that cause our emotional reactions but the way we think about these events [*tapping forehead*]. There are usually two styles of thinking that we bring to bear in focusing on our problems: one is rigid, the other is flexible.

PAULA: That seems plausible. I know colleagues at work with those thinking styles.

MICHAEL: Now the story. Two people are considering whether to ask their boss for help because their workloads are rapidly increasing. That's the situation or A. The first person has rigid beliefs, B, about the A, 'I must not ask my boss for help because if I do, this will mean I am weak and inadequate.' With that belief in mind, how do you think the person will feel and behave at C?

PAULA: Like me, anxious, panicky, keeping quiet.

MICHAEL: Now the second person has flexible beliefs, B, about the A, 'I want to ask my boss for help. There is no reason why I must not ask him. When I do ask for help, it just means that I'm a fallible person who is struggling with her workload, and that's all it means.' With that belief in mind, how do you think the person will feel and behave at C?

PAULA: Maybe a bit worried or maybe couldn't even care less but she would be asking for the help she needs without putting herself down for it. She's got more guts than me.

MICHAEL: So what's the point of the story?

PAULA: [*pointing at the whiteboard*] It's the way the person thinks at B about the situation that decides how they feel at C. I'm stuck feeling the way I do at C because I'm thinking rigidly at B about the situation at A. That's my ABC.

MICHAEL: Not quite. What is your rigid belief then?

PAULA: 'I must not ask my boss for help. If I do, this proves I'm weak and inadequate.' God, aren't I hard on myself?

MICHAEL: Let's hope not for much longer. Before we go on, can I just clarify something: are you weak and inadequate in your role as an interior designer or as a person if you ask for help?

[Self-depreciation can mean just the role or an aspect of a person; you should not automatically assume it refers to the person.]

PAULA: As a person. I do my best to avoid asking for help. It's a rule of mine.

MICHAEL: Maybe we can explore that rule later in counselling. So, what kind of belief would help you to achieve your goal of asking your boss for help?

PAULA: A flexible one.

MICHAEL: Can you express a flexible belief in your own words?

[It is best if your client puts her flexible (rational) belief in her own words rather than parrot a rational belief supplied by you as this latter belief is likely to carry less conviction for her than one that is self-constructed.]

PAULA: 'I want to ask my boss for help when I feel I need it. Asking for help means I'm a normal person, not a weak or inadequate one.' That sounds all right, doesn't it?

MICHAEL: Just one thing: what does being a 'normal person' mean to you?

[When some clients use this term, it just means they are going to be a little less hard on themselves which, in practice, really means that they are still strongly wedded to self-depreciation.]

PAULA: That we all need a little bit of help sometimes, don't we? A helping hand in troubled times.

MICHAEL: If you asked for quite a bit of help from your boss, would you still see yourself as 'normal'?

PAULA: Asking for a bit of help is all right, normal, but asking for a lot of help means I'm weak and inadequate.

MICHAEL: So you start off with what seems a flexible belief about asking for help, but if and when you go beyond 'a bit of help', you're back to putting yourself down; in other words, a return to rigid thinking [*client nods*]. OK. We can return to this issue later.

[As counselling progresses, I hope to teach Paula the REBC concept of self-acceptance, that is, never judge oneself, only one's actions; her current conception of 'normal' is self-limiting and ultimately self-defeating.]

Paula, like some clients, not only grasped the significance of the story but also applied it to her own situation: to reach her goal she needs to start replacing rigid beliefs with flexible ones (however, her view of what constitutes a flexible belief does not allow for much flexibility at the present time – it would be surprising if any client perceived immediately and fully that a flexible belief in REBC terms means adaptability to changing circumstances without accompanying self-depreciation).[5] Other clients, however, may understand your story but then need help to apply it to their own situation in order to uncover their irrational beliefs.

The Use of Questions to Assess Irrational Beliefs

This help comes in the form of open-ended and theory-driven questions. Open-ended questions encourage your client to think for herself about her belief system and its relationship with her emotional reactions at C.

Open-ended questions help you to determine how much REBC material your client has accurately retained, for example, 'Given your partner's ingratitude at A, what are you telling yourself at B to feel angry at C?' In our experience, the above question will often elicit an inference (assumption) rather than an irrational belief (demand), such as 'I think he's gone off me' as against 'He musn't treat me like this!' If this is the case, it is important to teach your client that, according to REBC theory, inferences are peripheral to emotional disturbance while irrational beliefs are central to it. Feedback can be sought to determine if your client has understood this crucial difference between inferences and beliefs and then the same question can be asked again; it is hoped that your client's reply will now focus on the demands she makes in this situation.

If the answer is the same or similar, then you will probably need to ask a theory-driven question. This is one derived from REBC theory and directs your client to the answer required, for example 'What demand are you making about your partner's ingratitude at A that leads you to feel angry at C?' Again in our experience, despite spoon-feeding the answer to your client, she might answer with a preference, such as 'I wish he wouldn't behave like that.' As with the distinction between inferences and beliefs, further teaching is required to emphasise to your client the difference in outlook between demands (rigid) and preferences (flexible).

Theory-driven questions seem to substantiate one of the major criticisms directed at REBC, namely, that you put words in your client's mouth. However, an ethical REB counsellor would make the ABCDE model of emotional disturbance and change explicit to her client and elicit her informed consent to proceed before fully involving her in the therapeutic process. In this way, your client has consented to have her attention drawn to 'musturbatory' (musts) thinking if she wants to learn this particular model of emotional problem-solving.

When your client does reveal her irrational beliefs, unlike Paula she may not see the immediate connection of B to C which you then need to make explicit – 'If you continue to demand that your partner must not show ingratitude and he continues to show it, then you will continue to make yourself angry. Can you see that connection?' Even if your client does see the B–C connection it does not automatically follow she will realise that moderating her thinking at B will lead to a moderation in her disturbed feelings at C – 'If you want to stop feeling angry at C, what needs to change first?' Establishing the B–C connection can be a difficult process for your client as she is, like many people, an habitual A–C thinker. Your client is now expected to start making a fundamental shift in her view of emotional causation: 'Events or others don't make me upset; I do', so patience and patient explanation are required from you.

Step 4: Examining Irrational and Rational Beliefs

Disputing, or D in the ABCDE model (see Figure 2.2), is not quarrelling with your client about her irrational beliefs but subjecting these beliefs to examination in order to test their validity. Both demand (rigid musts and shoulds) and conclusion (awfulising, low frustration tolerance or depreciation of self and/or others) components of an irrational belief are targets for examination; however, your client may not agree that both components are present in her belief or that one component is more strongly 'heard' than the other. If this is the case, your examination should be directed at the irrational component that has been acknowledged by your client or the one she wants to mainly focus on.

Examination is intended to encourage your client to develop a flexible or rational belief system in specific contexts, across situations or as a general philosophy of living depending on the degree of change your client wishes to embrace. Examination usually starts in specific contexts before taking, if clinically indicated, a wider view of your client's life and problems. Examination relies primarily on five points to help your client see the self-defeating nature of her irrational beliefs:

1 **Rigidity versus flexibility**. Rigid beliefs allow no other outcome than the one demanded and if this demand is not met, your client is left without options – 'I must not fail this exam. I will not tolerate failure!' Flexible beliefs emphasise the client's strong desire for goal-attainment but also acknowledge the possibility of setbacks and failures; if these occur, contingency plans are activated – 'I very much wanted to pass my exam but, unfortunately, I did not. Given this fact, I will resit my exam.'

2 **Extremism versus non-extremism**. Extremism in REBC means a tendency to think about ourselves, others and the world immoderately: cognitive balance or restraint is abandoned and thinking is pushed to its furthest limits in making judgements; for example a man who loses his job believes he is utterly worthless without one; a woman who falls out with her daughter concludes that her life is awful. Non-extremism

is based on a moderate outlook: arguments are balanced and judge-ments are made in the round: for example the man who loses his job now refrains from making his self-worth contingent upon having a job – 'I'm currently jobless, never worthless'; the woman who falls out with her daughter regrets that their relationship is now fraught with tension but her life is certainly not awful because of it.

3   **Logic**. The basic form of reasoning starts with a premise and reaches a conclusion derived from it. This form of reasoning is called deductive logic. An argument is deemed to be logical if it is impossible for the conclusion to be false if the premise is true. REBC argues, derived from its theory, that your client's irrational premises are false ('I must have the respect of my colleagues') and therefore the conclusion will also be false ('for without it, I'm no good') because there are no logical grounds to support unconditional musts and absolute shoulds or global evaluations of human worth. No matter how convincing your client's arguments may appear to be (e.g. enhanced well-being, greater job efficiency, higher productivity if she has their respect) there is still no logical basis for her must or self-depreciation.

Examination based on logic includes pointing out to your client 'that because something is more desirable, it does not logically follow that the world [or others] *must* provide what is desirable' (Walen et al., 1992: 160; emphasis in original). For example, 'Because you very much want the respect of your colleagues, how does it logically follow that you must have their respect?' Also, your client would probably not condemn others for failing to achieve their goals but unhesitatingly condemns herself for goal failure ('I'm no good'). Your client needs to explain this logical inconsistency to you as well as the double standard underpinning it (e.g. 'My goals are more important than theirs. That's why I can be understanding to them but not to myself').

4   **Empiricism**. This form of examination asks your client: 'Are your beliefs realistic? Do your beliefs correspond with the world as it actu-ally is?' Your client is required to provide evidence in support of her beliefs. REBC argues that rigid musts and absolute shoulds do not match empirical reality. For example, if I demand that I must have blue eyes instead of brown eyes, then my eye colour would change immedi-ately if the world bowed to my dictates. Your client would probably agree that such a demand was absurd, but then revert back to insisting that her demands are realistic, for example, 'I must have his love. What's wrong with that?' If your client was ruler of the universe, then

her demands would be obeyed without question; in this case, her partner could do no other than love her.

If your client condemns herself as a total failure, you can point out that if this was indeed true then all she could ever do is fail; so how did she manage to get up in the morning, get washed, dressed and fed, get the right bus, get to the session on time, etc.? Reality-testing your client's irrational beliefs helps her to see that her beliefs are inconsistent with empirical reality, that is, the latter does not change to accommodate her musts or adjust itself to reflect her self-depreciation.

5   **Pragmatism**. This line of enquiry focuses on the usefulness/helpfulness of subscribing to irrational beliefs, for example, 'Where is it going to get you holding on to the belief that you must always succeed?' Even though your client might respond that 'musts are motivating' and she has achieved considerable success in her life, this drive for success is now costing her dear in terms of her physical and psychological health. For many clients, pragmatism is the most effective form of examination in helping them to initiate change in their life as it graphically itemises the self-defeating consequences of irrational thinking.

Your client may cling tenaciously to her irrational beliefs, so you need to be non-dogmatically persistent in 'chipping away' at these beliefs with counter-arguments. Just asking standard disputing questions (e.g. 'Is that good logic?', 'Where's the evidence?' and 'Where's that belief going to get you?') often makes no impact upon your client, so creativity in the examination process is called for (Neenan and Dryden, 2002). For example, I (MN) saw a client who believed 'I'm worthless without a man in my life'; standard REBC arguments had no impact upon her until I asked her if she would teach that belief to her teenage daughter: 'Absolutely not. I don't want her to be as screwed up as I am.' What would she teach her daughter? 'That you are the same, worthwhile person whether or not you have a man in your life.' She decided to follow her own advice and therapeutic progress was made.

Socratic and Didactic Styles of Examination and When to Use Them

These are the two major styles of examination in REBC (Neenan and Dryden, 2000). Socratic examination involves asking questions that stimulate your client's thinking about the rigid/flexible, extreme/non-extreme, logical, empirical and pragmatic status of her beliefs, for example 'When you say that you must always be right, is that must always met? What are the consequences for you when it isn't?' Such questions guide your client to discover what REB counsellors already know, namely, there is no evidence to support irrational beliefs (presumably, if your client's musts were always met she would not need your services). Socratic examination can be an exacting and, at times, painful process for your client as she struggles to answer your questions because this may be the first time in her life that she has been required to inspect her beliefs in such detail.

Sometimes this question and answer approach will be unproductive (e.g. 'I have no idea why making demands is irrational. If you don't demand, you don't get!'). When this is the case, you can switch to a didactic format where you teach your client the REBC viewpoint on the subject under discussion (e.g. awfulising beliefs appeal to an alternative, non-existent reality where things should be less bad than they currently are). As with the B–C connection, you should ensure that your lectures are brief and clear and do not turn into opportunities to impress clients with your 'wisdom' or to ride a hobby-horse. The point of the lecture is to educate your client about REBC and then elicit feedback to determine if she has both understood and agreed with the points made in the lecture. Remember that your client can understand the REBC viewpoint without agreeing with it (REB counsellors want to hear their clients' doubts, reservations and objections in order to discuss them). Understanding without agreement is likely to result in little therapeutic progress for your client.

To help you decide which examination style is likely to be more appropriate in counselling, you can assess your client's intellectual abilities. An unreflective client might do better with a more didactic style while a psychologically-minded client might profit more from a mainly Socratic style. Though both forms of examination will be used in counselling, it is preferable to be much more Socratic than didactic in order to let your client's brain take the strain of effortful and independent thinking – do not do your client's thinking for her! Too much lecturing can encourage your client to slip into a passive role in counselling as she is spoon-fed the 'correct' REBC answers. A succession of 'hmms' and/or frequent nods usually indicates that your client's attention is elsewhere.

Paula

In the last section of dialogue, Paula pinpointed her irrational belief as 'I must not ask my boss for help. If I do, this proves I'm weak and inadequate.' This belief can be written on your whiteboard (if you have one) before an examination of it commences. Paula wanted to focus on the self-depreciation component of the irrational belief as 'this is where my mind often is':

MICHAEL: We are going to take a critical look at your belief to see if it stands up to inspection using five criteria. Let's start with the self-depreciation statement. Does that statement promote rigidity or flexibility in your thinking?

PAULA: Rigidity, undoubtedly.

MICHAEL: How?

PAULA: [*musing*] How . . . er . . . well, it doesn't allow me to see things in any other way. It's like I've got tunnel vision. I always come to the same conclusion about myself if I ask for help.

MICHAEL: Would you agree that it severely limits your problem-solving options?

PAULA: Definitely.

MICHAEL: Another criterion is extremism versus non-extremism. Extremism is when the person pushes his or her thinking too far in one direction and loses sight of what we might call moderate or balanced thinking. Would you say that your self-depreciation reflects extreme or non-extreme thinking?

PAULA: Obviously I'm an extremist thinker. It makes me sound like some wild-eyed revolutionary [*laughs*]. I remember one of my colleagues got some criticism from a client and he started calling himself useless and I said he was going over the top in his reaction. I'm a fine one to talk! I never thought about it like that before but I am extremist thinker when it comes to asking for help. I certainly wouldn't teach my children, if I ever get round to having any, this sort of thinking, 'Don't ask your teacher for help, it's a sign of weakness.' That's rubbish.

MICHAEL: Now let's look at the role of logic. In what way does it make sense to you to conclude that asking for help from your boss proves you are weak and inadequate?

PAULA: It doesn't make any sense.

MICHAEL: Surely there is some sense to it as you said earlier that not asking for help is a general rule you follow.

PAULA: On one level it doesn't make any sense and I wish that was the level that would prevail in my thinking but, on another level, it does make sense because my father used to say to me that being self-reliant was the goal in life.

MICHAEL: Did you make your father's logic your logic? [*Client nods.*] Now I'm not trying to attack your father, but do you think he talked sense about everything?

PAULA: Of course not. He wanted me to be able to stand on my own feet, be independent, but I think I've gone too far. Everybody can ask for help when they need it, so why not me? What makes me so special?

MICHAEL: How would you answer that last question?

PAULA: I'm not special. I don't want to be special.

MICHAEL: And if you followed the logic of that, when you did ask for help . . . what?

PAULA: I wouldn't see myself as weak and inadequate. I'd be asking for help and that's all it would mean.

MICHAEL: Another criterion is how realistic is your belief? Does reality reflect that you're weak and inadequate when you ask for help?

PAULA: What do you mean?

MICHAEL: What evidence can or would you point to and say, 'There, I told you so, I'm weak and inadequate because I've asked for help.'

PAULA: Well, I feel it's true.

MICHAEL: Just because you feel it, doesn't make it true. Feelings are not facts. What observable evidence can you point to?

PAULA: I don't know. You're asking me things I haven't thought about before.

MICHAEL: OK. Shall we think about these things now? [*Client nods.*] Have you asked your boss for help before?

PAULA: Once. Very reluctantly.

MICHAEL: When you asked for help, were you weak and inadequate from that point on as reflected in, for example, your work, comments from clients or colleagues? In other words, did the environment at work, the one outside of your head, reflect your belief about yourself.

PAULA: No.

MICHAEL: Can you expand on that?

PAULA: Hmm. If it was true, I suppose I wouldn't be able to function in a competent way any longer, I'd produce poor-quality work all the time. The clients would not want me to do any work for them. The company would probably get rid of me if I was that bad. It sounds silly when I really think about it. However, I am struggling with my workload though. Isn't that evidence?

MICHAEL: Evidence of what? Struggling with your workload could be proof that you need to ask for help at the present time, but not proof you are weak and inadequate. An appropriate coping strategy in the circumstances, could one say that?

PAULA: I suppose it could be a coping strategy. I hadn't thought of that.

MICHAEL: You see, we can look at the same evidence but come to different conclusions about it.

PAULA: Why can't I think like this?

MICHAEL: When people are emotionally disturbed, they usually look for evidence to support their negative beliefs rather than disprove them. I am encouraging you to weigh up the evidence in this situation in a dispassionate way instead of rushing to judgement about yourself, especially as there is a lack of evidence to support such a judgement. Now, the final criterion I want to discuss with you is pragmatism. Is your belief helping you to cope constructively with this situation?

PAULA: Definitely not. I know I need help, and if I don't ask for it I'll get really stressed out and take time off from work. I don't want to do that but I feel I'm getting close to that point. My belief is of no help whatsoever.

MICHAEL: So the belief isn't helpful but your boss is likely to be.

PAULA: [laughs] You could put it like that.

MICHAEL: Any comments on this initial examination of your irrational belief?

PAULA: Now that you've put it under the microscope, I can't see much purpose in holding on to it. If I'm to be completely honest, my belief sounds like a lot of old rubbish.

Examining an irrational belief will not, in itself, make your client rational. As DiGiuseppe observes:

> RE[BC] does not state that insight is sufficient for change. It is not sufficient to have the insight that one has irrational beliefs that are causing one's emotional disturbance, nor is it sufficient to have the insight that a particular irrational belief is irrational. Unless clients have new ideas to replace their old irrational beliefs, they are likely to cling to their irrational beliefs even though they are aware that the ideas are incorrect. (1991: 181)

You can explain to your client the REBC view of rationality which is based on flexible and non-extreme thinking. It is important that your client puts her rational beliefs into personally meaningful terms rather than being instructed by you to parrot REBC jargon which would lend support to the often-expressed criticism of REBC that it turns out clients who are 'rational robots'. A rational belief is not assumed to be so but is subjected to the same scrutiny as an irrational belief:

MICHAEL: When we were looking at the B–C connection [beliefs largely determine feelings – step 3] you said your rational belief was, and I quote, 'I want to ask my boss for help when I feel I need it. Asking for help means I'm a normal person, not a weak and inadequate one.' However, your definition of normal was severely limited: asking for a little help was okay, asking for a lot of help meant putting yourself down. Any change in that?

PAULA: Yes, I've been thinking about that. I want normal to mean that asking for help is OK in itself whatever the amount of help asked for. Obviously I wouldn't ask for help just for the sake of it, only when I really needed it.

MICHAEL: OK. Let's write your rational belief on the whiteboard, bearing in mind your new definition of normal, and apply the same five criteria to it. Now, is that belief rigid or flexible?

PAULA: It's flexible.

MICHAEL: In what way?

PAULA: Er . . . you're really making me think, aren't you? I think I'm going to go home with my brain aching.

MICHAEL: I want to be sure you really see the differences between rational and irrational beliefs.

PAULA: Okay, point taken. It's flexible because . . . it's not rigid. I don't really know why, to be honest.

MICHAEL: A flexible belief adapts to the reality, circumstances of a particular situation. It provides you with problem-solving options.

PAULA: Oh I see. My rational belief is flexible because when I need help it allows me to ask for it, unlike the irrational belief, and, best of all, I don't have to give myself a hard time for it.

MICHAEL: Is the belief extreme or non-extreme?

PAULA: It's non-extreme because it's balanced and moderate.

MICHAEL: In what way is it balanced and moderate?

PAULA: There you go again, making me stretch my brain! [*musing*] In what way . . . er . . . well, it's reasonable to ask for help and there's nothing wrong with doing that, but it is unreasonable to call myself names for doing something that everyone does.

MICHAEL: OK. Is the rational belief based on logic? Does it make sense in other words?

PAULA: It makes sense because I wouldn't condemn my colleagues for asking for help, so what's good enough for them is good enough for me. I can't think of anything else.

MICHAEL: That's fine. Is the belief realistic?

PAULA: Yes, and I'll tell you why before you ask me. Because I do need help at the present time, the evidence shows that, but the evidence also shows I'm still capable and competent in doing my job.

MICHAEL: And the help from your boss will help you to maintain those standards and maybe raise them.

PAULA: Good point. If I try to go it alone at the present time my standards will start to slip, which they're starting to do anyway because of all the stress I'm under.

MICHAEL: Lastly, pragmatism. Will this belief be of any help to you?

PAULA: Yes, because it will free me from this bloody mental straitjacket I've got myself into and then I can start putting things right at work and maybe other areas in my life too.

MICHAEL: Anything you would like to add to our discussion of your new rational belief?

PAULA: Yes, it sounds good in theory, but will it work in practice?

MICHAEL: Putting it into action is the next step.

The five tests applied to Paula's irrational and rational beliefs are not mandatory for every client – this would be a rigid application of REBC. It is important that you assess your client's intellectual and verbal abilities in order to determine how extensive the examination will be. In our experience, clients will usually quickly indicate which criterion or criteria (e.g. rigidity, pragmatism) is/are the most persuasive arguments in helping them to surrender their irrational beliefs and adopt rational beliefs. You should then focus on these arguments and abandon using the others. For some clients, structuring the examination in this formal way will be counterproductive as they are likely to react against being 'led by the nose'; in these circumstances, you can suggest that they undertake their own examination with you offering some additional ideas for their consideration.

Intellectual Insight and Emotional Insight: How to Believe in Your Gut What You Know in your Head

Paula's question, 'Will it work in practice?', is a familiar one in REBC. Once the initial phase of cognitive examination has been completed, your client can usually see the potential benefits of adopting rational ideas and giving up irrational ones. This awareness is often referred to as intellectual insight, that is, your client sees the theoretical advantages of a rational outlook in tackling her problems; however, this outlook has not been tested yet in those situations where she experiences her emotional problems. When rational ideas are tested in such situations, they often prove to be weak and ineffective in combating your client's entrenched irrational ideas.

Emotional insight is achieved when your client has forcefully and persistently disputed and acted against her irrational beliefs and argued in favour of and acted in support of her rational beliefs – you can only be sure that belief change has occurred when it is reflected in your client's behaviour. We might say that intellectual insight is 'I know these new beliefs make sense but don't believe it yet', while emotional insight is 'I know it and believe it.' This distinction between intellectual and emotional insight is also called the 'head–gut' split because clients often say 'I know it up here [tapping head] but don't feel it down there [prodding stomach].' You can anticipate that your client will experience this 'head–gut' split by initiating a discussion on the subject; this acts as a prelude to considering ways of deepening your client's conviction in her rational beliefs and weakening her conviction in her irrational beliefs. This is what I now do with Paula:

MICHAEL: Do you believe that changing your thinking will be a straightforward affair?

PAULA: I'm sure it won't be easy. Nothing has been so far. How difficult is it going to be then?

MICHAEL: Let me give you an example to explain what's involved. Do you write with your left or right hand?

PAULA: Right hand.

MICHAEL: Let's say you wanted to write with your left hand. Would it be a simple matter of swapping the pen from your right hand to your left hand?

PAULA: I shouldn't think so. I would have to practise lots and lots with the left hand to be able to write well with it.

MICHAEL: Would it feel strange and uncomfortable writing with the left hand and would you feel strong urges to revert to the right hand to make things easier, get back to normal?

PAULA: Yes. I'm sure that's all true.

MICHAEL: And what would you need to do to resist those urges and put up with the strangeness and discomfort of writing with your left hand?

PAULA: Well, focus on my goal and keep persisting until I felt writing with my left hand was natural and comfortable.

MICHAEL: Now, it's the same process with moving from irrational beliefs to rational ones.

PAULA: Persist with the rational beliefs until they feel more natural to me and keep on bashing away at the irrational beliefs until they lose their power over me, so to speak.

MICHAEL: That's part of it. You also need to act in support of the new ideas and act against the old ones. Thinking differently won't make much of a difference without supporting action.

PAULA: So if I've got the message, I need to give up this idea that I'm weak and inadequate if I ask my boss for help and I need to prove this to myself by asking him for help with my workload. It seems so straightforward when I say it like that.

MICHAEL: Believe it or not, it can be relatively straightforward sometimes. Let's now turn our attention to the homework assignment.

Step 5: Negotiating and Reviewing Homework Assignments

At the end of every session, your client should be prepared to carry out homework tasks in order to strengthen her nascent rational beliefs. Homework is the activity that your client carries out between sessions in order to put into practice the learning that has occurred in your office. Homework is the primary means by which your client develops competence and confidence in her developing role as a self-counsellor. Homework tasks fall into the following categories (they will be discussed in greater detail in Part 3):

- Cognitive. These tasks help your client to become more informed about the theory and practice of REBC and thereby help her to deepen her intellectual insight (knowledge) into her problems and the required methods to overcome them, e.g. reading self-help literature, listening to audiotapes of the sessions.
- Behavioural. These tasks are a key feature of REBC as your client learns to act against her disturbance-producing beliefs and in favour of her rational beliefs, for example, entering and remaining in previously

avoided social situations and accepting herself for any gaffes she might make. Behavioural tasks demonstrate to your client that she is achieving emotional insight (conviction) because she may doubt the efficacy of her new rational beliefs if she does not act upon them.

- Imagery. By using mental images or pictures as a form of rehearsal, your client can gain confidence that she will be able to carry out the assignment *in vivo*. Also, your client can use imagery to achieve an affective shift (from a disturbed to a non-disturbed feeling) through cognitive restructuring while vividly imagining an aversive situation. (It is important that your client does not alter the situation in any way in order to feel better; the only thing that is altered is her beliefs.)

- Emotive. These tasks are designed to engage fully your client's disturbed feelings in order to ameliorate them through the persistent and powerful challenging of her ingrained irrational ideas. For example, a client who makes herself angry when she is delayed or inconvenienced, forcefully reminds herself that it is, 'Tough! Learn to deal with it, not disturb yourself about it', in order to moderate her anger. As Yankura and Dryden observe: 'The emotions we experience . . . are influenced by the manner in which we talk to ourselves' (1994: 92).

Negotiating Homework Assignments

In negotiating homework tasks, you should keep the following important points in mind:

Ensure that the task follows on from the work done in the session

If the session focus has been on self-acceptance, then the homework will involve a task that will help to deepen your client's understanding of this concept (e.g. reading) or acting in a way that supports self-acceptance (e.g. speaking up in contexts where the client might incur criticism or disapproval).

Collaborate with your client

It is good practice to enlist your client's active collaboration when discussing possible homework tasks. In order to increase the likelihood that a particular assignment will be carried out, you should ensure that your client (a) sees the relevance to her problem in undertaking the assignment;

(b) agrees that carrying it out will help in the attainment of her desired goals; (c) has the requisite skills to execute the assignment; and (d) has some confidence in her ability to carry out the assignment (your client may have the skills but not necessarily the confidence to use those skills). Your client's compliance with homework assignments is further enhanced by establishing when, where and how often the particular assignment will be carried out.

Use the criterion of challenging, but not overwhelming (Dryden, 2002)

This refers to assignments that are sufficiently stimulating to promote therapeutic change, but not so daunting as to inhibit your client from actually carrying them out, such as in the case of a client who wants a relationship and is prepared to go to a singles bar but, at this stage, only to observe, not participate. What might be a challenging assignment to you is viewed as overwhelming by your client because she may see you as trying to push her too far, too fast, too soon (your goals for your client can be more ambitious than hers).

Assess and troubleshoot obstacles to homework completion

You can not only help your client to identify any obstacles that may serve as impediments to homework completion, but also devise methods for tackling them. For example, your client says she might not be able to find the time for the homework but would be able find the time if a pleasurable activity presented itself; you can suggest, and your client will probably reluctantly agree, to fit the homework into the pleasurable activity slot, thereby removing the 'not finding time' problem.

Negotiate homework assignments for a variety of purposes

Homework is not just used for disputing irrational beliefs and strengthening rational beliefs. Homework can be used at various points and for various purposes throughout the counselling sequence. Thus, homework assignments can be designed to help your client (a) identify her disturbed feelings at C; (b) pinpoint which aspect of the A she is most upset about; and (c) detect her irrational beliefs at B. In addition, homework tasks can also be used to educate your client about the ABCDE model by reading self-help books (bibliotherapy) or listening to audiotapes of REBC lectures.

Your client can also audiotape her counselling sessions and listen to them at home; she may get more out of a particular session by listening to it than she did from participating in it because, for example, she was upset in the session and information presented by you was poorly processed by her.

> MICHAEL: We're nearing the end of the session and it's time to discuss the homework task. What might be a relevant task based on the work we've done in the session?
>
> PAULA: Well, I want to ask my boss for help, take the plunge.
>
> MICHAEL: And the point of doing that is . . .?
>
> PAULA: To accept the fact that I need help at the present time with my workload and not to put myself down because of it.
>
> MICHAEL: When will you ask him?
>
> PAULA: This Thursday at our regular meeting.
>
> MICHAEL: Will any obstacles get in the way of doing that?
>
> PAULA: As I said before, this anxiety, panicky feeling that prevents me saying the words 'I need help.'
>
> MICHAEL: How can you tackle that?
>
> PAULA: Hmm. I can make my request for help the first item on the agenda instead of leaving it to the end because, if I do that, I probably won't ask him. I'll take a few slow, deep breaths and then go for it.
>
> MICHAEL: I'll give you a copy of the homework task so there shouldn't be any misunderstanding at the next session what you've agreed to do. OK?
>
> PAULA: That's OK. Wish me good luck.
>
> MICHAEL: Good luck.

Reviewing Homework Assignments

At the beginning of or early on in every session, homework should be reviewed. If you overlook homework review or carry it out in a perfunctory way, then you are communicating to your client the unimportance of homework in REBC – the very opposite of what needs to be communicated! In reviewing homework, the focus is on the learning that can be extracted from it, not the success or failure of the task.

Check that your client faced the critical A

If this was the agreed task, did your client actually face the critical A she wanted to confront? For example, your client's key worry is her anticipated inability to cope with the intense discomfort she will experience when trying to assert herself with her next-door neighbour by asking him to turn down his loud music. At the next session, she says she tried to do the task but when 'tried' is examined, she confesses 'I lost my nerve.' The next step is to identify the obstacles to task completion, such as, 'I don't think I could cope with the bad atmosphere that would be created between us if I confront him.' Your client can practise new arguments in the session (e.g. 'At least a bad atmosphere between us is not as noisy as loud music') before making another attempt at confronting the critical A in question.

Verify that your client changed B

When your client reports success in executing her homework assignments, you need to ascertain if this success was due to her (a) changing an irrational belief to a rational one in the presence of a troublesome A; (b) changing the A itself or an inference(s) about A; or (c) the use of distraction methods. If (b) or (c) were used, your client can be congratulated on her efforts, then you can point out the short-term effects of these methods. Practical solutions (i.e. changing A) or distraction methods are merely palliative as they do not require or encourage your client to change her disturbance-producing beliefs when A is faced. Encountering adverse A's is unavoidable and therefore your client's emotional problems will be continually reactivated unless they are dealt with. 'To change A or B: that is the question' – the former option offers respite from disturbance-producing thinking while the latter option removes such thinking. The usual clinical strategy in REBC is to change B before changing A.

However, it is important for you not to insist on this strategy and imply or state that changing A is the 'inferior' solution. REBC is a flexible approach to emotional problem-solving and therefore changing the A can be the primary clinical intervention. As Walen remarks about her own REBC practice: 'Over the years, I've found myself more and more frequently leaning in that direction [changing the A], especially in situations of chronic unhappy marriage or demoralized students or employees' (2002: 65).

Not carrying out homework assignments

If your client fails to carry out her agreed homework tasks, accept her as a fallible human being and help her to identify the reasons for this failure, for example, 'I need to know that doing the homework will help me to solve my problems.' Such reasons will need to be addressed in order to promote homework completion – 'Knowing how effective the homework will be in helping me to solve my problems comes after I've done it, not before I've done it.' You should be particularly alert to the presence of low frustration tolerance (LFT) beliefs: 'LFT is perhaps the main reason that clients do not improve after they have gained an understanding of their disturbance and how they create it' (Walen et al., 1992: 8).

Even though your client knows that doing the tasks will help her to reach her goals, her LFT beliefs 'shout down' this knowledge when she complains, for example, 'It's too much work. I shouldn't have to work this hard to change. I can't stand it!' You can point out to your client that her LFT maintains the status quo (emotional disturbance) while developing a philosophy of higher frustration tolerance (HFT), that is, enduring the discomfort and difficulties of executing goal-related tasks, changes the status quo.

If you experience difficulty in clarifying the reasons why your client did not carry out her homework assignments, you could ask her to fill out a form designed to identify possible reasons for her non-compliance (see Appendix 1).

Paula

At the next session of REBC, Paula's homework assignment was reviewed:

MICHAEL: The agreed task was to ask your boss for help. Did you carry that out?

PAULA: I did. It went well.

MICHAEL: In what way?

PAULA: He said why didn't I ask him for help if I needed it. I told him about my irrational belief – I was surprised how open I was with him – and how it gets in the way when I need help. He said that asking for help is a sign of strength, not weakness, because the person realises their limitations at that point. He said that if I don't ask for help when I need it, then my work suffers, which isn't good for business, and the company suffers if I take time off through stress. So, good advice. He's not going to give me any new work at the present time and he's going to provide guidance in managing my workload. I came out of the meeting greatly relieved. I expected to come out with my tail between my legs.

MICHAEL: What do you think you've learned from the homework task?

PAULA: It's really silly not to ask for help when you need it. There's no shame in it. It's a normal, natural human response. I think I'll remind myself of that every day until I get it firmly fixed up here [*tapping head*].

MICHAEL: Has change started then?

PAULA: Definitely, and I want more of it.

MICHAEL: Good. Now, let's look at the rest of the agenda items.

Step 6: Working Through

This refers to internalising a rational outlook, E in the ABCDE model. Grieger and Boyd describe working through as

> the heart of REBC. Helping clients work through their problems – that is, systematically giving up their irrational ideas – is where most of the therapist's energy and time are directed and where longlasting change takes place. Successful working through leads to significant change, whereas unsuccessful working through leads to no gain or to superficial gain at best. It is as simple as that. (1980: 122)

Suggest to Your Client Different Homework Assignments to Examine the Same Irrational Belief

REBC theory hypothesises that thoughts, feelings and behaviours are interdependent and interactive processes: namely, that each will have components of the other two. Therefore, the preferred and possibly optimal way of challenging an irrational belief and developing a rational alternative is through a multimodal strategy: cognitive, imaginal, behavioural and emotive assignments. Such a multimodal approach can help to keep your client interested in the change process.

Discuss the Non-Linear Model of Change

You can explain that change is a non-linear process in order to prepare your client for the difficulties which may lie ahead as she attempts to challenge her irrational beliefs in a variety of contexts. Your client is likely to experience both success and setbacks in tackling her problems. As these setbacks can usually be anticipated, ways of dealing with them can be devised and be ready to hand when needed (e.g. 'A setback only truly sets me back if I don't make an effort to learn from the experience').

Change in REBC involves your client making herself less, or much less, emotionally disturbed when faced with adverse events, but never undisturbable – our fallibility militates against such a goal being realised; so change is measured in relative, not absolute, terms:

1   Frequency – are your client's disturbed feelings experienced less frequently than before?
2   Intensity – when your client does experience disturbed feelings, are they less intense than before?
3   Duration – do your client's disturbed feelings last for shorter periods than before?

Your client can be encouraged to keep a log of her disturbed feelings and the situations in which they occur, so she can record emotional change using these three criteria. Sometimes your client can make herself disillusioned because of her perceived lack of progress in feeling less disturbed (e.g. 'Counselling isn't helping me. I just feel the same'). However, by keeping a log, she can usually pinpoint emotional and behavioural shifts that are more gradual than dramatic and this helps her to see that improvement is occurring now, not at some future, unspecified date which she awaits impatiently (e.g. 'When will I get better?'). In addition, your client may find it helpful to read the booklet entitled *How to Maintain and Enhance Your Rational Emotive Behaviour Therapy Gains* (Ellis, 1984b). This booklet contains many helpful suggestions that your client may use to facilitate her own working-through process. It is reprinted in Appendix 2.

Encourage Your Client to Become Her Own Counsellor

The ultimate aim of REBC is to help your client transform herself into a self counsellor. In order to assume this role, your client is required to take increasing responsibility in the counselling sessions for designing, executing and reviewing her homework assignments, using the ABCDE model to understand and tackle her emotional problems and selecting appropriate techniques to promote therapeutic change. Unless your client can carry out these functions in her own life at her own prompting, her gains from counselling are unlikely to be maintained in the long term.

If your client is successful in taking on this role, you should notice a corresponding decrease in your own level of activity (e.g. your client sets the agenda, uncovers her rigid and extreme thinking, shows how irrational beliefs are present in other areas of her life) which allows you to reconceptualise your role as a consultant, coach, mentor or adviser. Your client acting as a self-counsellor should, ideally, be lifelong.

To encourage your client to be more active in the problem-solving process, you can use short, probing questions to move your client through the ABCDE model:

* 'What happened at A?'
* 'How did you feel (or act) at C?'
* 'Can you pinpoint your critical A in this situation?'
* 'What were you telling yourself at B to feel (or act) that way at C?'
* 'What disputes (D) did you use to tackle your irrational belief?'
* 'Can you think of a relevant homework task to challenge that belief?'
* 'What rational belief would you like to hold?'
* 'What will you do to strengthen your rational belief?'
* 'Through internalizing that belief, what new effects (E) in terms of thoughts, feelings and behaviour are you experiencing?'

The more work you do for your client in the session, the less work she is likely to do for herself outside of it; therefore, do not colonise your client's brain and do her thinking for her: promote independent thinking.

Paula

Paula reminded herself every day that asking for help 'is a normal, natural human response'; the pressures of her workload were now easing since her meeting with her boss. However, even though she felt relieved by talking frankly to him about her worries, she often found herself dwelling on her old fear that asking for help equals weakness and inadequacy: 'What if my boss really thinks I'm no longer up to the job? What do my colleagues think about me? They probably know I've asked him for help.' I pointed out to her that the mental conflict between old and new ways of thinking about her problem would continue for some time – old ideas do not immediately 'surrender' when confronted with new ideas – but repeatedly thinking and acting in support of her new rational belief would hasten the weakening or disappearance of her old irrational belief. For example, she said there was no evidence to support her belief that her boss thought she 'was no longer up to the job' (she asked him) and her colleagues expressed support (they pointed out to her she was not the only one in the office who needed help from time to time).

Even if some colleagues had made unkind comments about her request for help, Paula could comfort herself with the fact that she had the last argument, that is, she did not have to agree with such comments because she no longer believed that asking for help from her boss was a sign of personal inadequacy – 'I'm just a normal, fallible person.' After several sessions of REBC, Paula felt much more settled at work: 'I really believe I'm becoming self-accepting on this issue, what you suggested I try and become.' Also, the 'must' in her thinking ('I must not ask my boss for help') had lost its 'grip' on Paula by her acting against it. As will be shown in Part 3, the learning and progress Paula made in one problem area did not automatically transfer to other related, problem areas, in that she struggled with accepting herself if she asked for help in other areas of her life.

In this part of the book, we have reviewed the rational emotive behavioural counselling sequence which outlines the six treatment steps when your client has a single problem. However, clients rarely have only one problem, and in Part 3 we outline the rational emotive behavioural counselling process which discusses treatment issues that emerge during the beginning, middle and ending stages of REBC and when your client has more than one problem.

Notes

1　When we refer in this book to the rational emotive behavioural counselling sequence, we mean the steps you need to take to help your client with a given problem. In the next part of the book, we will discuss the REBC process. By this we mean the entire counselling process from beginning to end.

2　The gender of your client in this book was determined as female by the toss of a coin.

3　We prefer the term 'examination' to 'disputing' as the former indicates a collaborative endeavour in scrutinising clients' beliefs while the latter suggests, and in unskilled hands often creates, the adversarial tensions found in a courtroom.

4　As noted in Part 1, A in the ABC model consists of two parts: first, the situational A which stands for a situation that can be described objectively by your client or agreed upon by neutral observers; second, the critical A is the key inference, in a series of inferences about the situational A, that triggers your client's irrational belief. However, some REB counsellors prefer to group all cognitive activity under B, while reserving A for a situation that can be described objectively.

5   Flexibility can have negative connotations for some clients (e.g. pliable, compliant, 'giving in'), so it is important that you ascertain your clients' idiosyncratic definitions of the term, such as 'Flexibility means that I'm supposed to give in every time my partner wants her own way. No thanks.' Flexibility does not mean yielding endlessly to others' demands but, instead, considering what options are available in any given situation and then making a choice in the light of one's goals for change.

Part 3

THE RATIONAL EMOTIVE BEHAVIOURAL COUNSELLING PROCESS

In this final part of the book, we will outline the rational emotive behavioural counselling process and consider how the counsellor's use of strategies and techniques differs at different stages of the process.

While it is impossible to differentiate clearly between different stages of the counselling process, for the sake of clarity we will consider the beginning, middle, and ending stages of counselling.

The Beginning Stage

Establish a Working Alliance

The first task for you as a rational emotive behavioural counsellor is to greet your client and to begin to establish a productive therapeutic alliance with him. This will normally involve discussing his reasons for seeking counselling help, his expectations for counselling, and correcting any obvious misconceptions he has about the counselling process. You will also want to deal with such practicalities as fees, and frequency and length of sessions. However, your main task at the outset is to encourage your client to talk about his concerns, initially in an open-ended way while you communicate your understanding of his problems. It is important that you show your client that you understand his concerns, demonstrate an unconditional acceptance of him as a person, and establish your credibility as an effective counsellor. In rational emotive behavioural counselling, establishing counsellor credibility is best done if you adopt a problem-solving approach to your client's concerns from the outset. In doing so, you should preferably communicate to your client that you intend to help him as quickly as possible and that you take seriously the problems for which he is seeking help. This means, as has been shown in Part 2, that you quickly come to an agreed understanding with your client concerning which of his problems you are both going to address first. In order to establish credibility with your client it is also important for you to provide him with a clear rationale which makes the purpose of your intentions clear. You need to be flexible at this point since clients differ concerning the degree to which they benefit from a problem-focused approach to counselling. You are advised to accommodate to your client's expectations on this point. With some clients, for example, you may need to explore with them, in detail, their life situations, and also perhaps the historical determinants of their problems, before adopting a problem-solving focus. With other clients, however, you may enhance the therapeutic alliance by becoming problem-focused from the beginning. Here, as elsewhere, we suggest that you show a high degree of flexibility in modifying your approach to take into account both the treatment expectations of your client and the preferred mode of practice in rational emotive behavioural counselling (that is, an early focus on problem-solving).

We have shown in Part 2 that there are six major steps that you need to follow in dealing with any one of your client's given problems. Here, we want to stress that it is important to adjust your mode of therapeutic participation according to the client with whom you are working. In doing so you will strengthen the working alliance. Thus, you may need to vary the pace of your interventions with different clients. Some clients think very quickly and will therefore respond to a fairly rapid intervention approach. Others, however, process information much more slowly and with these clients you need to reduce the speed at which you talk and the pace of your interventions. Since rational emotive behavioural counselling is first and foremost an educational approach to counselling, you should respect your client's pace and way of learning and adjust your therapeutic interventions accordingly. If you work quite slowly with a client who would respond better to a more rapid exchange, then that client may become frustrated and may conclude that you are not helping him quickly enough. However, another client may find that you talk too quickly and deal with concepts too rapidly, and consequently may experience confusion at the outset. Realise that it is basically your responsibility to tailor your therapeutic delivery to the client you have before you. Do not expect that your client, when confused because he does not understand the points you are making, will readily disclose this to you. Thus, like all good counsellors, you need to be alert to your client's non-verbal cues to gauge his level of understanding.

Also, bear in mind that at the beginning of the counselling process it is important to meet your client's preferences concerning your counselling style. Clients vary concerning the value that they place on different therapeutic styles. Some clients, for example, respond best to counsellors who are informal in therapeutic style, and who are self-disclosing and friendly. Other clients, however, will respond better to greater counsellor formality. Such clients are more concerned with the counsellor's expertise and value a more distant, 'professional' style.

My (WD) own approach to determining how best to meet clients' preferences concerning my therapeutic style is based on a number of factors. First, I have found it valuable in an initial session to ask clients questions concerning their prior experiences of receiving formal counselling and of being helped more informally with their psychological problems. In doing so, I focus the discussion on the factors that clients have found both helpful and unhelpful in such 'therapeutic encounters'. I also ask them directly which particular style they would like me to adopt with them. As Tracey (1984) has argued, it is important to meet clients' initial preferences for counsellor behaviour if one is to develop a productive therapeutic alliance with them. Other rational emotive behavioural counsellors obtain similar information from standard forms that they may use at the outset of counselling. Some employ, for example, Lazarus's (1981) 'Life History Questionnaire', which contains the following questions:

1   In a few words what do you think therapy is all about?
2   How long do you think therapy should last?
3   How do you think a therapist should interact with his or her clients?
4   What personal qualities do you think the ideal therapist should possess?

Despite the use of such questions, please realise that the issue of adjusting your therapeutic style according to the unique requirements of particular clients is very much a matter of trial and error.

Some counsellors are uneasy about changing their therapeutic style with different clients. However, bear in mind that in your daily life it is very likely that you vary your interactive style with different people. It is likely that you interact differently with your family, strangers you might encounter, colleagues at work, and dignitaries you may meet in a formal setting. So you are probably familiar with the concept of being flexible in interactive style. In the same way, we encourage you to adopt a stance of therapeutic flexibility and vary your counselling style according to the *productive* desires of your client. We stress the word productive here since, of course, not all clients' preferences for counsellor behaviour are necessarily therapeutic. In rational emotive behavioural counselling, for example, it is important to avoid doing all the therapeutic work for your clients, to avoid meeting your clients outside counselling sessions for social purposes, and to avoid letting your clients lie on a couch while encouraging them to free associate.

Teach the ABC's of REBC

Another task that you have at the outset of counselling involves teaching your client the rational emotive behavioural model of emotional disturbance. First, encourage your client to understand that his emotional problems are determined largely by his irrational beliefs rather than by the troublesome events in his life. Secondly, help your client to understand that in order to change his dysfunctional emotions he needs to examine the beliefs that he holds now, in the present, rather than engaging him in an overly long exploration of the historical determinants of such beliefs. However, as noted earlier, some historical exploration can be helpful, if only to strengthen the therapeutic alliance between you and your client. Thirdly, encourage your client to see that if he wants to gain lasting benefit from counselling he needs to put into practice what he learns during counselling sessions. This involves working repeatedly at examining his irrational beliefs and his rational beliefs and acting in ways that are consistent with the latter and inconsistent with the former. You will have to go over these three major REBC insights repeatedly before your client internalises them to the extent that he acts on them in his everyday life.

At this early stage of counselling your client is unlikely to be knowledgeable about the ABC's of REBC. You thus need to take a focused active-directive approach to helping your client to learn the rational emotive behavioural model of emotional disturbance. Wherever possible, encourage your client to think for himself by engaging him in a Socratic dialogue. Using this type of exchange, help him understand that his emotional problems are largely determined by his irrational beliefs. However, at times you will need to use a didactic style in teaching your client the ABC's of REBC. Whenever you do this at length, check whether or not your client has understood the points you have made (a point which we emphasised in Part 2).

Given that rational emotive behavioural counselling has an educational focus, it is important that your client is clear about what you are trying to teach him (either Socratically or didactically). Thus, it is important to remain focused on one problem at a time. Switching from problem to problem when your client has several emotional problems can be quite confusing for him and may interfere with the major points you wish your client to learn.

By the end of the initial stage, your client should have learned that it is his irrational beliefs that largely determine his emotional and behavioural problems. He should have had initial experience of identifying the irrational beliefs that underpin his initial target problem. He should be able to discriminate his rational beliefs from his irrational beliefs, and should have had some initial experience at questioning both beliefs, using the logical, empirical, and pragmatic arguments outlined in Part 2.

This learning should be reinforced by homework assignments. At this stage such homework assignments may involve your client reading specific chapters concerning the ABC's of REBC in one of the available REBT self-help books (for example, Dryden and Gordon, 1990; Ellis and Becker, 1982; and Ellis, 1988). In addition, you may ask your client to fill in one of the available rational-emotive self-help forms.

Deal with your Client's Doubts

Given that clients have a wide variety of preferences concerning what approaches to counselling may be helpful to them, you may find at this stage that some of your clients may express doubts concerning the usefulness of rational emotive behavioural counselling to helping them overcome their problems. One approach to handling such doubts is to encourage your client to persist with an open mind in using rational emotive behavioural methods of change for a given time period (for example, five sessions), at the end of which you will review his experiences in using the approach. If, at the end of this period, your client continues to be doubtful concerning the usefulness of rational emotive behavioural counselling to his problems, discuss his views concerning what type of counselling approach he thinks may be helpful to him. A judicious referral at this stage may be more helpful to your client than encouraging him to persist with an approach to counselling about which he has serious doubts.

The Middle Stage

By the middle stage of counselling, your client should have gained some experience at questioning the irrational beliefs which underpin his target problem and his alternative rational beliefs. Your client should have become accustomed to the idea that homework assignments are an important component of the rational emotive behavioural counselling process, and may have had some experience of changing his irrational beliefs to their rational alternatives. While it is desirable for you to keep on track with a given problem (namely, the target problem) and to help your client through the rational-emotive counselling sequence outlined in Part 2, this is not always possible.

When to Change Tack

When your client has several problems, one of his problems other than his target problem may become more pressing during the middle stage of counselling. While it may be desirable to persist with the initial target problem until your client has reached a reasonable level of coping on that problem, to ignore the client's desire to work on a different and, to him, more salient problem, may unduly threaten the working alliance and you should avoid this if possible.

In our experience, there are a number of good reasons to switch tack and to deal with a different client problem before he has attained the coping criterion (the point at which the client is able to cope) on the target problem. The first indication that a productive shift in problem emphasis is warranted is when the client reports a crisis with the new problem. Imagine, for example, that your client's initial target problem is public-speaking anxiety. If he reports a crisis, namely that he has been physically abused by a family member and is experiencing emotional distress about this, then it is important to switch and to deal with this new problem. However, having made the switch, encourage your client to remain with the second problem until he has gone through the rational emotive behavioural counselling sequence and has achieved the coping criterion.

A second indication that it is important to switch to a second problem is when your client becomes emotionally disturbed in the session about this second problem and cannot concentrate on work on the target problem. If you try to continue to help him with his initial target problem you will rarely succeed and you will create the impression that you are more concerned with following your approach to counselling than you are with being empathic and responsive to the client's experience. Once again, when you have switched to the second problem, help your client to reach the coping criterion on that problem by proceeding through the rational emotive behavioural counselling sequence.

A final reason to switch to a different problem before you have helped your client to reach the coping criterion on the initial target problem is when one of your client's other problems has become more pervasive than the target problem – that is, it pervades a greater number of areas of your client's life than does the target problem. Once you have switched to the new problem, again persist with it until your client has reached the coping criterion.

If your client has several problems and wishes to deal with different ones before he has attained the coping criterion on any one problem, give him a plausible rationale for remaining with one problem and for working on it until the coping criterion has been reached. If your client still wishes to switch between different problems even after hearing your rationale, then do so to preserve the therapeutic alliance. However, if you suspect that your client is switching between different problems in order to avoid dealing with any one problem, then put this forward as a hypothesis for further exploration with your client. Once again bear in mind that while you may prefer to help your client to reach the coping criterion on any one given problem before tackling a second or subsequent problem, you may have to be flexible to avoid unduly threatening the therapeutic alliance which by now you have established with your client.

Identify and Work on Core Irrational Beliefs

Whether you deal with your client's problems one at a time, switching from one to the other when the client has reached the coping criterion on any given problem, or whether you have to compromise this ideal way of working and switch from problem to problem in order to engage your client fully in counselling, it is important that you look for common themes among the irrational beliefs that underpin his problems. Thus, if your client has discussed public-speaking anxiety, procrastination, anxiety about approaching women, and fear of being criticised by his work superior, begin to form hypotheses concerning the presence of core irrational beliefs which may be common across these problems. Thus, in the example that we have given, it may be that your client's problems concern ego anxiety related to the need to be approved. If this is the case, then as you work on a number of these problems you may suggest to the client that there may be a similarity between these problems with respect to the underlying cognitive dynamics. However, guard against making the assumption that all of your client's problems can be explained with reference to one core irrational belief, since this is rare. More common is the clinical fact that your client may have two or three core irrational beliefs. These, rather than specific problems, should become the focus for therapeutic exploration and intervention during this middle stage of counselling.

Encourage your Client to Engage in Relevant Tasks

Your major goal during the middle stage of rational emotive behavioural counselling is to encourage your client to strengthen his conviction in his rational beliefs. This involves both you and your client using a variety of cognitive, emotive, imagery, and behavioural techniques which are all designed to encourage him to internalise his new rational philosophy.

Before discussing these techniques, however, it is important to note that as a counsellor you need to help your client:

1 to understand what his tasks are in counselling and how the execution of these tasks will help him to achieve his therapeutic goals;
2 to identify and overcome his doubts about his ability to execute his tasks;
3 to understand what your tasks are in rational emotive behavioural counselling and to see how your tasks relate to his tasks and his therapeutic goals;
4 to undertake tasks that he can realistically be expected to carry out;
5 to use therapeutic tasks in the sessions before you can expect him to put these into practice outside sessions;
6 to use techniques which are potent enough to help him to achieve his therapeutic goals.

Since the main burden of responsibility for promoting client change rests on your client carrying out homework assignments between sessions, it is important that you prepare him adequately to execute such assignments. Thus, you need to:

1 provide a persuasive rationale for the importance of executing home-work assignments in rational emotive behavioural counselling;

2 negotiate with your client suitable homework assignments rather than unilaterally suggest what these assignments should be;

3 negotiate assignments which are relevant to your client achieving his goals;

4 negotiate assignments which follow on naturally from what has been discussed in counselling sessions;

5 specify as fully as possible what these assignments will be, when your client is going to do them, and where and how he is going to execute them;

6 elicit a firm commitment from your client that he will execute these homework assignments;

7 encourage your client, whenever possible, to rehearse the particular homework assignment in the session. Your client is more likely to execute homework assignments successfully when he can picture himself doing so in imagery;

8 identify and overcome potential obstacles that may prevent your client from putting into practice particular homework assignments;

9 negotiate homework assignments which are not too time-consuming for your client;

10 suggest assignments which are challenging at a particular time for your client but not overwhelming for him.

Since the successful execution of homework assignments is such an important part of rational emotive behavioural counselling, it is very important that you check what your client's experiences were in executing these assignments:

– Ask your client to report what he learned or did not learn from carrying out the assignments.

– Reinforce his *success* at executing assignments and, where necessary, reinforce his *attempts* at executing these assignments.

– Identify and correct errors that your client made in carrying out his homework assignments.

– Identify, assess, and deal with your client's reasons for not attempting or not completing his homework assignments. In particular help him to question and change his resistance-creating irrational beliefs.

– Encourage him to re-do the assignment.

Major Counselling Techniques

In this section we will outline the major techniques that are used to help your client to internalise his newly acquired rational beliefs.

Cognitive Techniques The following cognitive techniques are used to promote belief change:

1   *Tape-recorded examination of beliefs.* Here your client records a sequence on audio tape where he plays both the role of his irrational self and his rational self. The goal of this technique is for him to ensure that his rational self persuades his irrational self that his rational beliefs are more logical, more consistent with reality, and will give him better results than his irrational beliefs.

2   *Rational coping self-statements.* Here your client repeatedly reminds himself of his rational beliefs as stated in short coping self-statements. You may encourage your client to write such statements on 5×3 cards which he can carry around with him and use as cue cards to remind himself of the suitable rational messages.

3   *Teaching REBC to others.* Here your client practises his new rational philosophy by teaching REBC to his friends. During this process he has an opportunity to defend his rational beliefs and to point out to others flaws in their logic.

4   *Semantic precision.* Here your client becomes aware of his use of language when this serves to perpetuate his irrational beliefs. In particular, you can encourage your client to identify such statements as 'I can't do X' and to replace this with 'I haven't yet done X.'

5   *DIBS (Disputing Irrational Beliefs).* DIBS is a structured form of questioning irrational beliefs that is particularly helpful in the middle stage of REBC. Here your client asks himself six questions and provides answers which are relevant to the irrational belief that he has targeted to challenge and change.

   (a)   What irrational belief do I want to question and surrender?

   (b)   Can I rationally support this belief?

   (c)   What evidence exists of the truth of this belief?

   (d)   What evidence exists of the falseness of this belief?

   (e)   What are the worst possible things that could actually happen to me if what I am demanding must not happen actually happens?

   (f)   What good things could happen or could I make happen if what I am demanding must not happen actually happens?

6 *Psycho-educational methods.* These involve your client reading the rational emotive behavioural self-help literature more extensively than in the beginning stage of REBC and listening to audio cassettes of REBC lectures on various themes.

7 *Referenting.* Referenting involves your client listing both the negative and positive referents of a particular concept such as 'procrastination'. This method is used particularly to counteract clients' tendencies to focus on the positive aspects of a self-defeating behaviour and to neglect its negative aspects. The purpose here is to encourage your client to focus on the negative aspects of self-defeating behaviours so as to provide him with an additional motivation to overcome such behaviour.

8 Further use of *cognitive homework forms* is suggested in the middle stage of rational emotive behavioural counselling. However, once your client has become skilled at completing such forms, he is encouraged to actively question both his irrational and rational beliefs without using the forms. Your client may be encouraged to keep using such forms, particularly when he experiences difficulty questioning his irrational beliefs in his head and when he begins to work on new problems.

Imagery Techniques The following imagery techniques are used to promote belief change:

1 *Rational-emotive imagery.* The main imagery technique that rational emotive behavioural counsellors use is rational-emotive imagery (Maultsby and Ellis, 1974). Here your client is encouraged to gain practice at changing his unhealthy negative emotion to a healthy negative emotion at C, while maintaining a vivid image of the negative event at A. In doing so, what he is in fact learning is to change his self-defeating emotion by changing his underlying irrational belief at B.

2 *Coping imagery.* These techniques are helpful in encouraging your client to picture himself carrying out a productive behaviour in real life before in fact he actually does so.

3 *Time projection.* Here, for example, your client may state that a particular event would be 'terrible' if it occurred. You can indirectly challenge this belief by temporarily going along with this evaluation while helping your client to picture what life might be like at increasing

intervals in the future after the 'terrible' event has occurred. In this way, you are indirectly encouraging your client to change his irrational belief when he comes to understand that he can experience happiness again after the 'terrible' event has occurred and that he can either continue to pursue his original goals or develop new ones.

Emotive-evocative Techniques   These techniques encourage your client to fully engage his emotions in the change process while still having as your major goal helping him to identify, question, and change his irrational beliefs.

1   *Humorous exaggeration methods.*   These can be used to encourage your client to see the amusing aspects of his irrational beliefs. Let us suppose that your client is anxious that other people might learn something 'shameful' about him. You could take this to a humorous and absurd conclusion by showing him that not only will these people actually find out about his 'shameful' secret, but that so will everybody else in the country and it will be headline news in the daily newspapers for months. It is important to bear in mind that this use of humour should be directed at your client's ideas rather than at the client himself. Humour should be used sparingly and not with clients who would not consider such behaviour to be a legitimate part of a counsellor's role. Here, as elsewhere, it is important to bear in mind the importance of maintaining a productive working alliance when considering the use of humour.

2   *Rational humorous songs.*   The purpose of rational humorous songs is again to help your client to take himself seriously but not too seriously. Ellis (1987a) has written a number of rational humorous songs and encourages his clients to sing them at moments when they might otherwise make themselves unduly psychologically disturbed. An example of one follows:

> *Perfect Rationality*
> Some think the world must have a right direction
> And so do I! And so do I!
> Some think that with the slightest imperfection
> They can't get by – And so do I!

For I, I have to prove I'm superhuman
And better far than people are!
To show I have miraculous acumen –
And always rate among the Great!

Perfect, perfect rationality
Is, of course, the only thing for me!
How can I ever think of being
If I must live fallibly?
Rationality must be a perfect thing for me!

3   *Counsellor self-disclosure.*   Another way of encouraging your client to internalise a new rational philosophy is to disclose not only how you as a counsellor have experienced a similar problem in the past, but also how you overcame it. Thus, I (WD) sometimes tell my clients how I overcame my anxiety about having a stammer and therefore stammered less. First, I disclose how I used to make myself anxious by telling myself: 'I must not stammer, I must not stammer, it would be terrible if I were to stammer.' I then disclose how I changed this belief by disputing it and replacing it by the idea 'While I don't want to stammer, it's not the end of the world if I do.' I also mention that I practised this philosophy while deliberately speaking up at public meetings at every opportunity. In this example, I not only tell how I overcame a problem similar to my clients' by disputing my irrational belief; I also show them how important it is to do so while acting according to the rational belief.

4   *Stories, mottoes, parables, and aphorisms.*   You can use such stories, for example, to reinforce a rational message and to show your client that there are other sources of rationality apart from more standard disputing methods. Thus, for example, I often tell the story of the Buddhist monk who, while travelling with his apprentice, meets by a river bank a young girl who wishes to cross to the other side. According to his religion, however, the monk is not supposed to talk to the woman, let alone touch her, and yet he carries her across the river and puts her down on the opposite bank. After walking several miles further, his apprentice cannot contain himself and asks the monk why he carried the woman when his religion forbids him to do so. The Buddhist monk replies that his apprentice is still carrying her (that is,

in his mind). This story is particularly helpful with clients who believe that there are absolute laws which forbid you to do something under all conditions.

5   *The use of force and vigour in examining irrational and rational beliefs.* Ellis (1979) has argued that the use of force and vigour in the belief-examination process is particularly helpful in encouraging clients to internalise rational philosophies. You can encourage your client to repeat rational self-statements very forcefully or to engage in a very forceful dialogue with himself, particularly on audio cassette where he can encourage his rational self to challenge very forcefully the arguments made by his irrational self.

6   *Rational role reversal.*   Once your client has shown some skill at questioning his irrational beliefs, you can adopt the position of devil's advocate in the counselling session, and present irrational arguments to encourage him to defend, and thus strengthen, his newly acquired rational philosophy. In doing so, you can also help to identify vulnerable points in your client's thinking, particularly when he demonstrates faltering acceptance of the rationality of his new beliefs.

7   *Shame-attacking exercises.*   These are particularly helpful for clients who are ashamed about exposing some weakness in public. In using such exercises, you encourage your client deliberately to act 'shamefully' in public so as to gain practice at accepting himself for his 'shameful' behaviour and to tolerate the ensuing discomfort. However, it is important to safeguard against your client acting illegally or harming himself or other people. Encouraging your client to break minor social rules is particularly helpful in this respect (for example, wearing bizarre clothes designed to attract public attention).

Behavioural Techniques   Critics often claim that rational emotive behavioural counselling neglects the use of behavioural assignments. However, this has never been true although the previous name of the counselling approach (rational-emotive therapy) did give some the wrong impression that behavioural methods were not employed. On the contrary, rational emotive behavioural counsellors consider that unless clients put into practice, through action, what they learn in counselling sessions, then they will find it difficult to internalise a new rational philosophy. So you can encourage your client to use activity homework assignments whenever possible (for example, to confront fears and to court discomfort) while at the same time encouraging him to question his irrational beliefs cognitively. This simultaneous use of cognitive and behavioural methods places REBC firmly in the cognitive-behavioural tradition of counselling.

Other behavioural techniques that you can use include anti-procrastination exercises where you encourage your client to push himself to start tasks sooner rather than later, while putting up with the discomfort of undertaking unpleasurable tasks. Also, like their behavioural colleagues, rational emotive behavioural counsellors advocate the judicious use of rewards and penalties to encourage clients to undertake uncomfortable assignments in the pursuit of their long-range goals. As Ellis (2002) has noted, the use of stiff penalties is found to be especially useful with clients who prove to be particularly resistant on certain issues.

Whenever possible, you should encourage your client to confront his fears fully rather than gradually. This is because full exposure methods encourage clients to overcome their philosophy of low frustration tolerance (LFT) more than do gradual exposure methods. Indeed, Ellis (1983c) has argued that the latter may even reinforce your client's LFT in that they may encourage him to believe, 'I must avoid making myself quite uncomfortable at all costs.' However, compromises on this issue often have to be made. Thus, when our clients find *in vivo* desensitisation methods based on flooding principles *too* 'overwhelming' for them at a given time, we encourage them to carry out an assignment that is challenging for them rather than one that they can do very comfortably.

REBC also advocates the use of skills training methods (for example, assertion training). However, these are best used together with cognitive restructuring methods rather than on their own. It is this conjoint use of cognitive and behavioural techniques that distinguishes rational emotive behavioural counsellors from their behavioural colleagues.

Additional Issues   You will frequently have no way of knowing in advance which assignments your client will find helpful, and therefore you should use a trial-and-error approach to find this out. Also, discuss with your client your intention to discover which techniques work and do not work for him, otherwise he may become discouraged when he uses a technique that does not lead to progress.

Since your main goal during this stage is to encourage your client to internalise a new rational philosophy, you and your client need to determine reasons for therapeutic change. Ideally, your client should be effecting change by questioning his irrational beliefs rather than by changing his inferences about life events or the events themselves or by changing his behaviour. If you discover that your client has demonstrated therapeutic change without changing his irrational beliefs, reinforce his efforts but point out to him the importance of changing his irrational beliefs. Remind him of the rational emotive behavioural hypothesis that long-term change is best achieved by philosophic change.

Deal with Obstacles to Change

It is during the middle stage of rational emotive behavioural counselling that clients show most resistance to change. Assuming that your client has understood that his irrational beliefs do determine his emotional and behavioural problems and that he has gained some initial success at questioning his irrational beliefs, it is likely that his resistance to change can be attributed to his philosophy of low frustration tolerance (LFT). Frequently, clients do not follow through on their initial successful change because they believe that 'Change must not be difficult' or 'I should not have to work so hard in counselling.' It is very important for you to be alert to the possibility that your client may have a philosophy of LFT about change, and if so you need to help him to question and change the irrational beliefs implicit in such a philosophy. Otherwise, these beliefs will interfere with your client's attempts to internalise a new rational philosophy.

Maultsby (1984) has argued that change itself can be an uncomfortable experience for clients. He refers to a state called 'cognitive-emotional dissonance' during which clients feel 'strange' as they work at strengthening their conviction in their rational beliefs. Encourage your client to accept that this feeling of 'strangeness' is a natural part of change and if necessary dispute any ideas that he must feel natural and comfortable all of the time. Grieger and Boyd (1980) have called this concern the 'I won't be me' syndrome.

You will encounter a minority of clients who internalise the theory of REBC as a body of knowledge, but who will not work towards putting this knowledge into practice. Such clients are often very knowledgeable about the theory and can quote extensively from various REBC books, but often have an implicit philosophy of LFT which stops them from putting their knowledge into practice. They may also believe that their knowledge is sufficient for them to effect lasting emotional and behavioural changes. As with other clients, the ideas which stop them from putting their knowledge into practice need to be identified, challenged, and changed.

Encourage your Client to Maintain and Enhance his Gains

It is in the middle stage of counselling that your client will experience greatest variability in the progress he makes, sometimes going forward, sometimes backsliding. As a result, you need to help him stay fully engaged in counselling by helping him (a) to deal with set-backs; (b) to maintain his progress and later, (c) to enhance his gains. Ellis (1984b) has written an excellent pamphlet on this issue which is reproduced in Appendix 2. We refer you to this for the variety of points made and suggest that you give a copy to your clients when the issues raised by Ellis become salient.

Encourage your Client to Become his own Counsellor

Another important task that you have as a rational emotive behavioural counsellor in the middle-to-late stage of counselling is to encourage your client to work towards becoming his own counsellor. We noted in the previous section on the beginning stage of rational emotive behavioural counselling that you will often have to take an active-directive stance in helping your client to learn the ABC's of REBC and to understand why his irrational belief is self-defeating and the rational alternative is more constructive. As you move into the middle stage of counselling, you will need to review such points. However, the more you do so, the more you should encourage your client to take the lead in the exploration, particularly in the middle-to-late stage of counselling.

When you first discuss a particular problem with your client, be active and directive, but the more you work on this problem, gradually reduce the level of your directiveness and encourage your client to practise self-counselling. As you work together with your client on a particular problem over the course of counselling, help him to internalise the rational emotive behavioural problem-solving method. Encourage him to learn to identify troublesome emotions and behaviours, help him to relate these to particular activating events, and from there to identify his major core irrational beliefs. Then encourage him to question these beliefs for himself and to develop plausible rational alternatives to these beliefs. Your client's major task during this stage of counselling is to weaken his conviction in his core irrational beliefs and strengthen his conviction in his core rational beliefs.

Not only should you encourage your client to internalise the REBC process of change, but you should also encourage him to look for links between his problems, particularly those that involve core irrational beliefs. Your goal should be to help your client to identify his core irrational beliefs across a number of settings and to question and change these beliefs. As noted above, while you should reduce the level of your directiveness as you help your client to deal with a particular problem, you may have to go back to becoming active and directive when the focus of therapeutic exploration shifts to a new problem. However, as a major goal of this stage is to encourage your client to begin to become his own counsellor, you should endeavour, even when working on a new problem, to encourage your client to take the lead in the exploration of this new problem.

During this stage of counselling you should increasingly use Socratic dialogue to encourage your client to do most of the work and you should keep didactic teaching to a minimum. In particular, you should use short, probing, Socratic questions to check on your client's progress. Thus, when your client discusses his experiences in dealing with his problem between sessions you may ask questions such as the following:

> 'How did you feel?'
> 'What was going through your mind?'
> 'How did you question that?'
> 'How could you have questioned that?'
> 'Did you believe the new rational belief?'
> 'Why not?'
> 'What could you believe instead?'
> 'How would you know that this belief was true?'
> 'If you believe that, how would you act?'
> 'Could you try that for next week?' – and so on.

When your client responds successfully to your decreased level of directiveness over a period of weeks, then you may begin to start thinking about working towards termination (see next section).

The Ending Stage

The question of ending rational emotive behavioural counselling arises when your client has made significant progress towards overcoming the problems for which he originally sought counselling and has shown evidence that he has been able to utilise the rational emotive behavioural problem-solving method in approaching his problems. Discussion about termination may be raised by either you or your client. When you both decide that you will work towards termination of counselling this may be done either by decreasing the frequency of sessions over time or by setting a definite termination date. During this stage, you can usefully encourage your client to anticipate future problems and to imagine how he would apply the skills which he has learned during the rational emotive behavioural counselling process to these problems. Your goal should be to encourage your client to view himself as his own major source of solving problems and discussion should centre on how he can apply his problem-solving skills in a variety of settings.

Clients who have done well during rational emotive behavioural counselling may have ambivalent feelings towards ending the process. You may need, for example, to assess whether or not your client believes that he needs your ongoing help. This may be expressed by your client casting doubts on his ability to cope on his own or by him reporting a relapse before termination. The best way of dealing with your client's belief, 'I must have the ongoing support of my counsellor, because I cannot cope on my own' is as follows. First, encourage him to question this irrational belief and the rational alternative in the usual way. Then, urge him to conduct an experiment to see whether or not it is true that he cannot cope on his own. Help him to specify which aspects of his life he thinks he cannot cope with on his own and then encourage him to test this out as a homework assignment.

Whether you are working with your client towards a phased or definite ending, build in well-spaced-out follow-up sessions so that you and your client can monitor his future progress. In one respect, there is no absolute end to the rational emotive behavioural counselling process because in most cases you would probably want to encourage your clients to contact you for further help if they have struggled on their own for a reasonably long time to put into practice the rational emotive behavioural problem-solving method without success.

When rational emotive behavioural counselling has been successful and you are working towards termination with your client, bear in mind that what has been a significant relationship for your client and perhaps for you is coming towards an end. Thus, it is highly appropriate for both you and your client to feel sad about the dissolution of this relationship. We believe it is important for you to encourage your client to express this sadness and in doing so he may express feelings of gratitude for your help. While you may wish to encourage your client to attribute most of his progress to his own efforts (this is undoubtedly true since he had the major responsibility for carrying out homework assignments between sessions), if you believe you have done a good job then it is appropriate for you to say this to your client.

Sometimes your client may offer you a gift in recognition for the help that you have given him. Our own practice is to accept a gift with gratitude as long as its value in monetary terms is not highly disproportionate to the occasion. Appropriate gifts in this regard are perhaps a bottle of alcohol, some flowers or a small figurine. Some clients, however, do have difficulty saying goodbye and difficulty in experiencing and expressing sadness about the end of a relationship. They may, for example, cancel their final session or try to introduce a light-hearted tone into the final session. While extending counselling at this stage for too long is not to be recommended, we do suggest that in such instances you first look for possible irrational beliefs that your client may have about saying goodbye and about experiencing and expressing sadness concerning losing an important relationship. Then, encourage him to use his skills to identify, question, and change the relevant irrational beliefs that underpin these difficulties.

The Rational Emotive Behavioural Counselling Process: Paula

In Part 2, we introduced Paula, a 30-year-old woman who worked as an interior designer, who was very reluctant to ask her boss for help with her heavy workload. Asking for help was, in Paula's view, proof of her weakness and inadequacy. We outlined the rational emotive behavioural counselling sequence that I (MN) implemented in dealing with Paula's problem. In this part of the book, I (MN) will draw together my counselling work with Paula to show the REBC process in action.

When I first met Paula I asked her what she wanted from counselling: 'I've got a problem with asking for help.' This 'problem with asking for help' was related to her workplace difficulties in managing an ever-increasing workload and her reluctance to speak to her boss about this problem. I asked her if she had been in counselling before and she replied with a firm 'no'. She thought that being in counselling was a sign of weakness and toyed with the idea of cancelling her appointment, but finally decided that 'talking things through' with someone removed from her life might be helpful in breaking the log-jam in her thinking about asking for help. I asked her what kind of interpersonal approach she might best respond to and she said a 'direct, no-nonsense approach'. She said that if I behaved in a 'touchy-feely, namby-pamby' way, seemed fixated on her childhood or blamed her parents for her problems, she would terminate counselling.

I informed her that my usual manner was to be direct with clients, stay in the here and now in terms of problem-solving and encourage clients to take responsibility for both owning their problems and dealing with them, but I would not censor myself just because she might not like what I had to say or threaten to leave counselling. This was her first taste of the 'direct, no-nonsense' approach she wanted. After this airing of our viewpoints, I explained briefly the REBC model of emotional disturbance and change and sought her permission, which she gave, to teach it to her.

She then asked the ever-recurring client question: 'How long will it take?' I replied that it depended on the severity or complexity of her problem, the degree of acceptance of the REBC model, how ambitious were her goals, the amount of effort she was prepared to expend in order to achieve those goals and my own skill in guiding her through the problem-solving process (each client usually presents new challenges for the counsellor). As this was not the precise answer she was looking for, we agreed to a trial period of six weekly sessions to determine if REBC would be of help to her. I was reasonably confident that she would take to the active-directiveness of REBC and would be eager to become her own self-counsellor.

Her immediate problem focus was on the intense anxiety she would experience when asking her boss for help (she did not specify or point to other problems she wanted to discuss, so a problem list was not drawn up at this stage). The cognitive core of her anxiety was that asking her boss for help meant she was weak and inadequate as a person. Her initial goal was to find some way of avoiding asking for help but I was not prepared to agree to this goal as I would be supporting her self-depreciation beliefs about asking for help. This would make the goal counter-therapeutic (Persons, 1989). After some discussion, she agreed to the therapeutic goal of asking her boss for help and seeing it as a normal response in times of trouble, not an occasion for self-denigration. The irrational and goal-blocking belief identified for examination and modification was: 'I must not ask my boss for help. If I do, this proves I'm weak and inadequate.' Paula wanted to focus on the 'weak and inadequate' part of her irrational belief as this 'I hear loud and clear'. She responded well to the examination process and I pressed her, when necessary, to provide more detailed replies to my questions when her answers were unclear or short.

The rational belief that she developed to aid goal-attainment was: 'I want to ask my boss for help when I feel I need it. Asking for help means I'm a normal person, not a weak and inadequate one' (this was Paula's statement of self-acceptance). She would need to remind herself forcefully and repeatedly of this belief if she was to start internalising it and weakening her irrational belief. I kept pointing out that asking for help was not the problem, but the meaning she attached to it was. She said that not asking for help was a general rule she followed and that she might also want to modify it in other areas of her life.

At the end of the second session, Paula said that her homework would be to ask her boss for help, 'take the plunge' as she called it. Her boss responded positively to her request for help and she felt relieved that nothing 'terrible' had happened. However, this relief was soon followed by 'What if?' anxious thinking, such as, 'What if my boss really thinks I'm not up to the job?', 'What if my colleagues think I am weak and inadequate?' I suggested a twofold strategy to use on this issue: look for evidence to confirm or disconfirm her 'what ifs?' (the evidence she found was disconfirmatory) and as an added safeguard to assume the worst – her boss and colleagues did think these things about her – and learn to cope with it by choosing what to believe about herself, for example 'I don't agree with their opinion of me. I can't control what they think, only my own thoughts.'

Paula agreed with this reasoning but insisted that self-acceptance would not prevent her losing her job if her boss was right about her. This observation triggered a chain of catastrophic thoughts about, for example, losing her professional credibility, not being able to find another job, incurring large debts, becoming dependent on others. I decided not to venture into these areas because discussing coping plans to tackle these catastrophic outcomes would pull us away from our primary focus, namely, Paula learning to accept, not denigrate, herself when asking her boss for help: 'We need to stay looking at present problems, not speculating about possible future ones.' She agreed with the rationale underpinning my decision (we could look at these issues later in counselling if she wanted to; she never did). In order to strengthen her self-acceptance, Paula reminded herself every day that asking for help 'is a normal, natural human response'. In this way, she was able to reduce considerably the frequency, intensity and duration of her self-depreciation and spend more time where it belonged: managing her workload.

Another area that Paula wanted to look at was her relationship with her boyfriend; more specifically, her inability to ask him for help or comfort when she felt she needed it (the same irrational belief was present in this situation as it had been at work). In order to encourage Paula to work towards becoming her own counsellor, I asked her how she could transfer what she had learnt from one context (her boss) to another related context (her boyfriend). I did not assume a 'snowball effect' (Frisch, 1992), that her learning in one context would automatically generalise to other contexts. She was unsure how to transfer her learning. She provided an example of coming home from work after a particularly stressful day at work and wanting a cuddle from her boyfriend but did not ask for one because 'I didn't want to appear as a weak, pathetic, cry baby. You know, the kind of woman who needs a strong man to lean on.' She said she had nothing against 'a nice kiss and cuddle' except when she was feeling vulnerable – precisely the time when she might need it the most, I suggested.

The bottom line in this situation was, as at work, equating asking for help or comfort with weakness and inadequacy. At this point she grasped the transfer of learning, that is, to accept herself for asking for comfort from her boyfriend when she felt vulnerable. The 'what ifs' began to resurface ('What if he does see me as weak and needy?' 'What if I start crying as he's holding me?'). Again the strategy was twofold: look for evidence to support or undermine her 'what ifs' (she said she knew from his behaviour and comments that he did not see her in this way) and then assume the worst anyway to strengthen her self-acceptance, that is, if he does see her in this way, she does not have to agree with him – his evaluation of her did not have to become her self-evaluation. Also, crying was not the problem but, as usual, the negative meaning she attached to it.

After several sessions of counselling, Paula said she was warming to the idea of being both a personal scientist, that is, reality-testing her thoughts and beliefs, and a 'doom-monger':

> I imagine people pointing at me and saying, "We always knew you were weak and inadequate. The truth is finally out.' I feel down at first, but then I strike

back and declare: 'Too bad! Think what you want.' Then my mood lifts. If the
worst ever came to the worst, I could come through it.

This 'doom-mongering' was Paula practising rational-emotive imagery
(REI; Maultsby and Ellis, 1974) in which a client is encouraged to experience her situationally related disturbed feelings and then ameliorate these
feelings by changing her beliefs about the situation. Paula practised REI on
a daily basis for several weeks before phasing it out as 'I'm getting bored
with it. I just see the worst happening as now being just unfortunate,
nothing else.' She found Paul Hauck's book on self-acceptance, *Hold Your
Head up High* (1991), especially helpful in increasing her understanding of
this concept. As Paula was pleased with her progress, she wanted to continue counselling beyond the agreed six sessions.

Paula was moving from intellectual insight into overcoming her problems (knowing about self-acceptance) to emotional insight about
problem-solving (internalising self-acceptance). She had already asked her
boss for help and her boyfriend for a cuddle 'when I'm stressed out'; now
she wanted to extend self-acceptance to other areas of her life (she was
transferring her learning to other contexts without any prompting from
me – a good sign for becoming a self-counsellor). These other areas were
telling a few selected friends and her father that she was in counselling: 'I
would have previously seen that as the ultimate disgrace – counselling is for
weaklings.' The friends she told were surprised by her revelation and
curious to know why 'super-self-reliant' Paula needed counselling. She said
she explained her reasons without worrying what they might think about
her. However, one comment from a friend, 'How the mighty have fallen',
left her smarting. When, in the session, we examined her reaction, she said
that the comment 'made me seem like a hypocrite. I felt weak and pathetic
with her looking at me in that superior way. Who cares about self-
acceptance? Why did I want to put myself through that? I am weak and
pathetic.' Paula was surprised by the strength of her reaction but it under-
scored the point I had been repeatedly making, namely, that irrational
beliefs are usually weakened rather than eradicated by constant challenging and they are often reactivated at times of emotional stress; therefore,
she needed to be on her guard for their reappearance in her thinking and
to take immediate and forceful action against them when they appeared.

On reflection, Paula said that her friend's comment was accurate: 'The
sting of truth. I suppose I did deserve it. I was always banging on about
sorting your own problems out. Counselling was for losers. All that kind of

stuff.' Her father was dismissive about counselling, as she expected, but she stood her ground and told him of the perils of compulsive self-reliance (such as feeling isolated from friends and colleagues, emotional exhaustion) and the benefits of counselling: 'I've learnt it's no crime to ask for help. I'm more rounded as a better person for it.'

After ten sessions of REBC, Paula indicated that she was near to terminating counselling. She suggested two more sessions on a fortnightly basis. In the penultimate session, we looked at relapse-prevention, that is, dealing with anticipated future situations that might trigger a lapse (a partial return to a problem state) or relapse (a complete return to a problem state). Paula said that her warning signs of 'slipping back would be when I become emotionally twitchy because I'm pushing myself too hard to make sure I'm on top of things. You know, the old fear of not showing any weakness to the world.' If and when these warning signs appeared, she said she would slow down and remind herself that she did not have to prove anything to the world or herself (how well this strategy worked would be assessed during follow-up appointments).

In the last session, we reviewed her progress as a self-counsellor and I asked her what key lessons she would take away from counselling: 'The most important lesson is being self-reliant within the context of compassionate self-acceptance; so I can ask for help or comfort when necessary without feeling I've let myself down because of it. Thank you for teaching me that. I never want to lose sight of that.' Paula said that she wanted to tell me something she found funny in retrospect: when she first came to counselling she had sternly told me that if I behaved in a 'touchy-feely, namby-pamby way' she would immediately leave: 'Even in counselling I had to prove how strong and tough I was. What a case I am.' I replied that I guessed what she was up to and, initially, overplayed the no-nonsense approach to keep her in counselling. We both laughed at our 'games' and then said goodbye. Paula agreed to follow-up appointments in six and twelve months' time in order to monitor her progress. She could contact me before these scheduled appointments if she ran into difficulties she could not deal with herself.

At the six month follow-up, Paula was maintaining her gains from counselling. She had some episodes of 'emotional twitchiness' but said she 'slapped down' her irrational beliefs when they 'started to cause trouble'. She adopted the phrase, 'There I go again', to remind herself she was beginning to slip back into her old ways of thinking, feeling and behaving related to excessive self-reliance. She said she was getting more out of her work and social relationships since she had 'opened up'. She reported that she now enjoyed having a support network – once a 'ghastly phrase' to her – and that when she came across 'got-to-be-strong-at-all-times' types, she explained to them the rational ideas she had learnt to help her get out of her 'self-created trap'. Paula said that teaching others, if they were interested, helped to strengthen her own rational ideas.

At the twelve-month follow-up session, which was brief and conducted on the telephone, Paula said she was fine and her old problem was now 'a very distant echo'.

Appendix 1

POSSIBLE REASONS FOR NOT COMPLETING SELF-HELP ASSIGNMENTS

(TO BE COMPLETED BY CLIENT)

The following is a list of reasons that various clients have given for not doing their self-help assignments during the course of counselling. Because the speed of improvement depends primarily on the amount of self-help assignments that you are willing to do, it is of great importance to pinpoint any reasons that you may have for not doing this work. It is important to look for these reasons at the time that you feel a reluctance to do your assignment or a desire to put off doing it. Hence, it is best to fill out this questionnaire at that time. If you have any difficulty filling out this form and returning it to the counsellor, it might be best to do it together during a counselling session. (Rate each statement by ringing 'T' (True) 'F' (False). 'T' indicates that you agree with it; 'F' means the statement does not apply at this time.)

1 It seems that nothing can help me so there is no point in trying.   T/F
2 It wasn't clear, I didn't understand what I had to do.   T/F
3 I thought that the particular method the counsellor had suggested would not be helpful. I didn't really see the value of it.   T/F
4 It seemed too hard.   T/F
5 I am willing to do self-help assignments, but I keep forgetting.   T/F
6 I did not have enough time. I was too busy.   T/F

7 If I do something the counsellor suggests I do it's not as
good as if I come up with my own ideas.   T/F
8 I don't really believe I can do anything to help myself.   T/F
9 I have the impression the counsellor is trying to boss me
around or control me.   T/F
10 I worry about the counsellor's disapproval. I believe that
what I do just won't be good enough for him/her.   T/F
11 I felt too bad, sad, nervous, upset (underline the
appropriate word(s)) to do it.   T/F
12 It would have upset me to do the homework.   T/F
13 It was too much to do.   T/F
14 It's too much like going back to school again.   T/F
15 It seemed to be mainly for the counsellor's benefit.   T/F
16 Self-help assignments have no place in counselling.   T/F
17 Because of the progress I've made, these assignments
are likely to be of no further benefit to me.   T/F
18 Because these assignments have not been helpful in
the past, I couldn't see the point of doing this one.   T/F
19 I don't agree with this particular approach to counselling.   T/F
20 OTHER REASONS (please write them).

Appendix 2

HOW TO MAINTAIN AND ENHANCE YOUR RATIONAL EMOTIVE BEHAVIOR THERAPY GAINS

ALBERT ELLIS PhD
Albert Ellis Institute
New York City

If you work at using the principles and practices of rational emotive behavior therapy (REBT), you will be able to change your self-defeating thoughts, feelings and behaviors and to feel much better than when you started therapy. Good! But you will also, at times, fall back – and sometimes far back. No one is perfect and practically all people take one step backwards to every two or three steps forward. Why? Because that is the nature of humans: to improve, to stop improving at times, and sometimes to backslide. How can you (imperfectly!) slow down your tendency to fall back? How can you maintain and enhance your therapy goals? Here are some methods that we have tested at the Albert Ellis Institute in New York and that many of our clients have found quite effective.

How to Maintain your Improvement

1. When you improve and then fall back to old feelings of anxiety, depression, or self-downing, try to remind yourself and pinpoint exactly what thoughts, feelings, and behaviours you once changed to bring about your improvement. If you again feel depressed, think back to how you previously used REBT to make yourself undepressed. For example, you may remember that:

(a)   You stopped telling yourself that you were worthless and that you couldn't ever succeed in getting what you wanted.
(b)   You did well in a job or in a love affair and proved to yourself that you did have some ability and that you were lovable.
(c)   You forced yourself to go on interviews instead of avoiding them and thereby helped yourself overcome your anxiety about them.

Remind yourself of thoughts, feelings, and behaviours that you have changed and that you have helped yourself by changing.
2.   Keep thinking, thinking and thinking rational beliefs (rBs) or coping statements, such as: 'It's great to succeed but I can fully accept myself as a person and enjoy life considerably even when I fail!' Don't merely parrot these statements but go over them carefully many times and think them through until you really begin to believe and feel that they are true.
3.   Keep seeking for, discovering, and disputing and challenging your irrational beliefs (iBs) with which you are once again upsetting yourself. Take each important irrational belief – such as, 'I have to succeed in order to be a worthwhile person!' – and keep asking yourself: 'Why is this belief true?' 'Where is the evidence that my worth to myself, and my enjoyment of living, utterly depends on my succeeding at something?' 'In what way would I be totally acceptable as a human if I failed at an important task or test?'

Keep forcefully and persistently disputing your irrational beliefs whenever you see that you are letting them creep back again. And even when you don't actively hold them, realize that they may arise once more, bring them to your consciousness, and preventively – and vigorously! – dispute them.
4.   Keep risking and doing things that you irrationally fear – such as riding in elevators, socializing, job hunting, or creative writing. Once you have partly overcome one of your irrational fears, keep acting against it on a regular basis. If you feel uncomfortable in forcing yourself to do things that you are unrealistically afraid of doing, don't allow yourself to avoid doing them – and thereby to preserve your discomfort forever! Often, make yourself as *un*comfortable as you can be, in order to eradicate your irrational fears and to become unanxious and comfortable later.
5.   Try to clearly see the difference between healthy negative feelings – such as those of sadness, concern, remorse, and disappointment, when you do not get some of the important things you want – and unhealthy negative feelings – such as those of depression, anxiety,

guilt, and shame, when you are deprived of desirable goals and plagued with undesirable things. Whenever you feel *over*concerned (panicked) or *unduly* miserable (depressed), acknowledge that you are having a statistically normal but a psychologically unhealthy feeling and that you are bringing it on yourself with some dogmatic *should*, *ought*, or *must*. Realize that you are invariably capable of changing your unhealthy (or *must*urbatory) feelings back into healthy (or preferential) ones. Take your depressed feelings and work on them until you *only* feel sadness and regret. Take your anxious feelings and work on them until you *only* feel concerned and vigilant. Use rational-emotive imagery to vividly imagine unpleasant activating events before they happen; let yourself feel unhealthily upset (anxious, depressed, enraged, or guilty) as you imagine them; then work on your feelings to change them to appropriate emotions (concern, sadness, healthy anger, or remorse) as you keep imagining some of the worst things happening. Don't give up until you actually do change your feelings.

6.   Avoid self-defeating procrastination. Do unpleasant tasks fast – today! If you still procrastinate, reward yourself with certain things that you enjoy – for example, eating, vacationing, reading, and socializing – only *after* you have performed the tasks that you easily avoid. If this won't work, give yourself a severe penalty – such as talking to a boring person for two hours or burning a hundred dollar bill – every time that you procrastinate.

7.   Show yourself that it is an absorbing *challenge* and something of an *adventure* to maintain your emotional health and to keep yourself reasonably happy no matter what kind of misfortunes assail you. Make the uprooting of your misery one of the most important things in your life – something you are utterly determined to steadily work at achieving. Fully acknowledge that you almost always have some *choice* about how to think, feel, and behave; and throw yourself actively into making the choice for yourself.

8.   Remember – and use – the three main insights of REBT that are outlined in *Reason and Emotion in Psychotherapy* (Ellis, 1994):

Insight No. 1:   You largely *choose* to disturb yourself about the unpleasant events of your life, although you may be encouraged to do so by external happenings and by social learning. You mainly feel the way you think. When obnoxious and frustrating things happen to you at point A (activating events), you consciously or unconsciously *select* rational beliefs (rBs) that lead you to feel concerned, sad and remorseful and you also *select* irrational beliefs (iBs) that lead you to feel anxious, depressed, and guilty.

Insight No. 2: No matter how or when you acquired your irrational beliefs and your self-sabotaging habits, you now, in the present, *choose* to maintain them – and that is why you are *now* disturbed. Your past history and your present life conditions importantly *affect* you; but they don't *disturb* you. Your present *philosophy* is the main contributor to your *current* disturbance.

Insight No. 3: There is no magical way for you to change your personality and your strong tendencies to needlessly upset yourself. Basic personality change requires persistent *work and practice* – yes, *work and practice* – to enable you to alter your irrational beliefs, your unhealthy feelings, and your self-destructive behaviours.

9. Steadily – and unfrantically! – look for personal pleasures and enjoyments – such as reading, entertainment, sports, hobbies, art, science, and other vital absorbing interests. Take as your major life goal not only the achievement of emotional health but also that of real enjoyment. Try to become involved in a long-term purpose, goal, or interest in which you can remain truly absorbed. For a good, happy life will give you something to live *for*; will distract you from many serious woes; and will encourage you to preserve and to improve your mental health.

10. Try to keep in touch with several other people who know something about REBT and who can help go over some of its aspects with you. Tell them about problems that you have difficulty coping with and let them know how you are using REBT to overcome these problems. See if they agree with your solutions and can suggest additional and better kinds of REBT disputing that you can use to work against your irrational beliefs.

11. Practise using REBT with some of your friends, relatives and associates who are willing to let you try to help them with it. The more often you use it with others, and are able to see what their iBs are and to try to talk them out of these self-defeating ideas, the more you will be able to understand the main principles of REBT and to use them with yourself. When you see other people act irrationally and in a disturbed manner, try to figure out – with or without talking to them about it – what their main irrational beliefs probably are and how these could be actively and vigorously disputed.

12.   When you are in rational emotive behavioral individual or group therapy, try to tape record many of your sessions and listen to these carefully when you are in between sessions, so that some of the REBT ideas that you learned in therapy sink in. After therapy has ended, keep these tape recordings and play them back to yourself from time to time, to remind you how to deal with some of your old problems or new ones that may arise.

13.   Keep reading REBT writings and listening to REBT audio and audio-visual cassettes, particularly *Humanistic Pyschotherapy* (Ellis); *A Guide to Personal Happiness* (Ellis and Harper); *A New Guide to Rational Living* (Ellis and Becker); *Overcoming Procrastination* (Ellis and Knaus); *Overcoming Depression* (Hauck); and *A Rational Counseling Primer* (Young). Keep going back to the REBT reading and audio-visual material from time to time, to keep reminding yourself of some of the main rational emotive behavioural findings and philosophies.

How to Deal with Backsliding

1.   Accept your backsliding as normal – as something that happens to almost all people who at first improve emotionally and who then fall back. See it as part of your human fallibility. Don't feel ashamed when some of your old symptoms return; and don't think that you have to handle them entirely by yourself and that it is wrong or weak for you to seek some additional sessions of therapy and to talk to your friends about your renewed problems.

2.   When you backslide look at your self-defeating *behaviour* as bad and unfortunate; but work very hard at refusing to put *yourself* down for engaging in this behaviour. Use the highly important REBT principle of refraining from rating *you*, your *self*, or your *being* but of measuring only your *acts*, *deeds*, and *traits*. You are always a *person who* acts well or badly – and never a *good person* nor a *bad person*. No matter how badly you fall back and bring on your old disturbances again, work at fully accepting yourself *with* this unfortunate or weak behaviour – and then try, and keep trying, to change your behaviour.

3.   Go back to the ABCs of REBT and clearly see what you did to fall back to your old symptoms. At A (activating event), you usually experienced some failure or rejection once again. At rB (rational belief) you probably told yourself that you didn't *like* failing and didn't *want* to be

rejected. If you only stayed with these rational beliefs, you would merely feel sad or remorseful. But when you felt disturbed again, you probably then went on to some irrational beliefs (iBs), such as: 'I *must* not fail! It's *horrible* when I do!' 'I *have to* be accepted, and if I'm not that makes me an *unlovable worthless person!*' Then, after convincing yourself of these iBs, you felt, at C (emotional consequence) once again depressed and guilty.

4. When you find your irrational beliefs by which you are once again disturbing yourself, just as you originally used disputing (D) to challenge and surrender them, do so again – *immediately* and *persistently*. Thus, you can ask yourself, 'Why *must* I not fail? Is it really *horrible* if I do?' And you can answer: 'There is no reason why I *must* not fail, though I can think of several reasons why it would be highly undesirable. It's not *horrible* if I do fail – only distinctly *inconvenient.*' You can also dispute your other irrational beliefs by asking yourself, 'Where is it written that I *have* to be accepted? How do I become an *unlovable, worthless person* if I am rejected?' And you can answer: 'I never *have to be* accepted, though I would very much *prefer* to be. If I am rejected, that makes me, alas, a *person who* is rejected this time by this individual under these conditions, but it hardly makes me an *unlovable, worthless person* who will always be rejected by anyone for whom I really care.'

5. Keep looking for, finding, and actively and vigorously disputing your irrational beliefs which you have once again revived and that are now making you feel anxious or depressed once more. Keep doing this, over and over, until you build intellectual and emotional muscle (just as you would build physical muscle by learning how to exercise and then by *continuing* to exercise).

6. Don't fool yourself into believing that if you merely change your language you will always change your thinking. If you neurotically tell yourself, 'I *must* succeed and be approved' and you sanely change this self-statement to, 'I *prefer* to succeed and be approved,' you may still really be convinced, 'But I really *have to* do well and *have got to be* loved.' Before you stop your disputing and before you are satisfied with your answers to it (which in REBT we call E, or an effective philosophy), keep on doing it until you are *really* convinced of your rational answers and until your feelings of disturbance truly disappear. Then do the same thing many, many times – until your new E (effective philosophy) becomes hardened and habitual – which it almost always will if you keep working at arriving at it and re-instituting it.

7.   Convincing yourself lightly or 'intellectually' of your new effective philosophy or rational beliefs often won't help very much or persist very long.
Do so very *strongly* and *vigorously*, and do so many times. Thus, you can
powerfully convince yourself, until you really *feel* it: 'I do not *need* what I
want! I never *have to* succeed, no matter how greatly I *wish to* do so!' 'I
can stand being rejected by someone I care for. It won't *kill* me – and I *still*
can lead a happy life!' '*No* human is damnable and worthless – including
and especially *me*!'

How to Generalize from Working on One Emotional Problem to Working on other Problems

1.   Show yourself that your present emotional problem and the ways in
which you bring it on are not unique and that virtually all emotional and
behavioural difficulties are created by irrational beliefs (iBs). Whatever
your iBs are, moreover, you can overcome them by strongly and persistently disputing and acting against these irrational beliefs.
2.   Recognize that you tend to have three major kinds of irrational
beliefs that lead you to disturb yourself and that the emotional and
behavioral problems that you want to relieve fall into one of these three
categories:

(a)   'I *must* do well and *have to* be approved by people whom I find
        important.' This iB leads you to feel anxious, depressed, and self-
        hating; and to avoid doing things at which you may fail and avoiding
        relationships that may not turn out well.
(b)   'Other people *must* treat me fairly and nicely!' This iB contributes to
        your feeling unhealthily angry, furious, violent, and over-rebellious.
(c)   'The conditions under which I live *must* be comfortable and free from
        major hassles!' This iB tends to create your feelings of low frustration
        tolerance and self-pity; and sometimes those of unhealthy anger and
        depression.

3.   Recognize that when you employ one of these three absolutistic
musts – or any of the innumerable variations on it that you can easily slide
into – you naturally and commonly derive from them other irrational conclusions, such as:

(a) 'Because I am not doing as well as I *must*, I am an incompetent worthless individual!' (Self-depreciation).

(b) 'Since I am not being approved by people whom I find important, as I *have to be*, it's *awful* and *terrible*!' (Awfulizing).

(c) 'Because others are not treating me and fairly as nicely as they *absolutely should* treat me, they are *utterly rotten people* and deserve to be damned!' (Other-depreciation).

(d) 'Since the conditions under which I live are not that comfortable and since my life has several major hassles, as it *must* not have, I can't stand it! My existence is a horror!' (Low Frustration Tolerance).

(e) 'Because I have failed and got rejected as I *absolutely ought not* to have done, I'll *always* fail and *never* get accepted as I *must* be! My life will be hopeless and joyless forever!' (Overgeneralizing).

4.   Work at seeing that these irrational beliefs are part of your *general* repertoire of thoughts and feelings and that you bring them to many different kinds of situations that are against your desires. Realize that in just about all cases where you feel seriously disturbed and act in a distinctly self-defeating manner you are consciously or unconsciously sneaking in one or more of these iBs. Consequently, if you get rid of them in one area and are still emotionally disturbed about something else, you can always use the same REBT principles to discover your iBs in the new area and to eliminate them there.

5.   Repeatedly show yourself that it is almost impossible to disturb yourself and to remain disturbed in *any* way if you abandon your absolutistic, dogmatic *shoulds*, *oughts*, and *musts* and consistently replace them with flexible and unrigid (though still strong) *desires* and *preferences*.

6.   Continue to acknowledge that you can change your irrational beliefs (iBs) by rigorously (not rigidly!) using the scientific method. With scientific thinking, you can show yourself that your irrational beliefs are only theories or hypotheses – not facts. You can logically and realistically dispute them in many ways, such as these:

(a)   You can show yourself that your iBs are self-defeating – that they interfere with your goals and your happiness. For if you firmly convince yourself, 'I *must* succeed at important tasks and *have to* be approved by all the significant people in my life,' you will of course at times fail and be disapproved – and thereby inevitably make yourself anxious and depressed instead of concerned and sad.

(b)   Your irrational beliefs do not conform to reality – and especially do not conform to the facts of human fallibility. If you always *had* to succeed, if the universe commanded that you *must* do so, you obviously *would* always succeed. And of course you often don't! If you invariably *had* to be approved by others, you could never be disapproved. But obviously you frequently are! The universe is clearly not arranged so that you will always get what you demand. So although your desires are often realistic, your godlike commands definitely are not!

(c)   Your irrational beliefs are illogical, inconsistent, or contradictory. No matter how much you *want* to succeed and to be approved, it never follows that therefore you *must* do well in these (or any other) respects. No matter how desirable justice or politeness is, it never *has to* exist.

Although the scientific method is not infallible or sacred, it efficiently helps you to discover which of your beliefs are irrational and self-defeating and how to use factual evidence and logical thinking to rid yourself of them. If you keep using scientific analysis, you will avoid dogma and set up your hypotheses about you, other people, and the world around you so that you always keep them open to change.

7.   Try to set up some main goals and purposes in life – goals that you would like very much to reach but that you never tell yourself that you absolutely must attain. Keep checking to see how you are coming along with these goals; at times revise them; see how you feel about achieving them; and keep yourself goal-oriented for the rest of your days.

8.   If you get bogged down and begin to lead a life that seems too miserable or dull, review the points made in this pamphlet and work at using them. Once again: if you fall back or fail to go forward at the pace you prefer, don't hesitate to return to therapy for some booster sessions.

References

Bard, J.A. (1980) *Rational-Emotive Therapy in Practice*. Champaign, IL: Research Press.

Beck, A.T. (1976) *Cognitive Therapy and the Emotional Disorders*. New York: International Universities Press.

Beutler, L.E. (1983) *Eclectic Psychotherapy: A Systematic Approach*. New York: Pergamon.

Bordin, E.S. (1979) 'The generalizability of the psychoanalytic concept of the working alliance', *Psychotherapy: Theory, Research and Practice*, 16: 252–60.

Cormier, W.H. and Cormier, L.S. (1985) *Interviewing Strategies for Helpers*. 2nd edition. Monterey, CA: Brooks/Cole.

Crawford, T. and Ellis, A. (1989) 'A dictionary of rational-emotive feelings and behaviors', *Journal of Rational-Emotive and Cognitive Behavior Therapy*, 7(1): 3–27.

DiGiuseppe, R. (1988) 'Thinking what to feel', in W. Dryden and P. Trower (eds), *Developments in Rational-Emotive Therapy*. Milton Keynes: Open University Press.

DiGiuseppe, R. (1991) 'Comprehensive cognitive disputing in RET', in M.E. Bernard (ed.), *Using Rational-Emotive Therapy Effectively: A Practitioner's Guide*. New York: Plenum Press.

Dryden, W. (1986) 'Language and meaning in RET', *Journal of Rational-Emotive Therapy*, 4: 131–42.

Dryden, W. (1987) 'Theoretically-consistent eclecticism: humanising a computer "addict"', in J.C. Norcross (ed.), *Casebook of Eclectic Psychotherapy*. New York: Brunner/Mazel.

Dryden, W. (1996) 'Rational emotive behaviour therapy', in W. Dryden (ed.), *Handbook of Individual Therapy*. London: Sage.

Dryden, W. (1999) *Rational Emotive Behaviour Therapy: A Personal Approach*. Bicester, Oxon: Winslow Press.

Dryden, W. (2002) *Fundamentals of Rational Emotive Behaviour Therapy: A Training Handbook*. London: Whurr.

Dryden, W., DiGiuseppe, R. and Neenan, M. (2003) *A Primer on Rational Emotive Behavior Therapy*. 2nd edition. Champaign, IL: Research Press.

Dryden, W., Ferguson, J. and Hylton, B. (1989) 'Beliefs and inferences – a test of a rational-emotive hypothesis: 3. On expectations about enjoying a party', *British Journal of Guidance and Counselling*, 17(1): 68–75.

Dryden, W. and Gordon, J. (1990) *Think Your Way to Happiness*. London: Sheldon Press.

Ellis, A. (1962) *Reason and Emotion in Psychotherapy*. New York: Lyle Stuart.

Ellis, A. (1976) 'The biological basis of human irrationality', *Journal of Individual Psychology*, 32: 145–68.

Ellis, A. (1979) 'The issue of force and energy in behavioral change', *Journal of Contemporary Psychotherapy*, 10(2): 83–97.

Ellis, A. (1980) 'Rational-emotive therapy and cognitive behavior therapy: similarities and differences', *Cognitive Therapy and Research*, 4: 325–40.

Ellis, A. (1983a) 'Failures in rational-emotive therapy', in E.B. Foa and P.M.G. Emmelkamp (eds), *Failures in Behavior Therapy*. New York: Wiley.

Ellis, A. (1983b) 'How to deal with your most difficult client: you', *Journal of Rational-Emotive Therapy*, 1(1): 3–8.

Ellis, A. (1983c) 'The philosophic implications and dangers of some popular behavior therapy techniques', in M. Rosenbaum, C.M. Franks and Y. Jaffe (eds), *Perspectives in Behavior Therapy in the Eighties*. New York: Springer.

Ellis, A. (1984a) 'The essence of RET – 1984', *Journal of Rational-Emotive Therapy*, 2(1): 19–25.

Ellis, A. (1984b) *How to Maintain and Enhance your Rational Emotive Behavior Therapy Gains*. New York: Institute for Rational-Emotive Therapy.

Ellis, A. (1985) 'Expanding the ABC's of rational-emotive therapy', in M.J. Mahoney and A. Freeman (eds), *Cognition and Psychotherapy*. New York: Plenum.

Ellis, A. (1987a) 'The use of rational humorous songs in psychotherapy', in W.F. Fry, Jr. and W.A. Salameh (eds), *Handbook of Humor in Psychotherapy: Advances in the Clinical Use of Humor*. Sarasota, FL: Professional Resource Exchange Inc.

Ellis, A. (1987b) 'The evolution of rational-emotive therapy (RET) and cognitive behavior therapy (CBT)', in J.K. Zeig (ed.), *The Evolution of Psychotherapy*. New York: Brunner/Mazel.

Ellis, A. (1988) *How to Stubbornly Refuse to Make Yourself Miserable About Anything – Yes, Anything!* Secaucus, NJ: Lyle Stuart.

Ellis, A. (1989) 'Is rational-emotive therapy (RET) "rationalist" or "constructivist"?', in W. Dryden (ed.), *The Essential Albert Ellis: Seminal Writings on Psychotherapy*. New York: Springer.

Ellis, A. (1994) *Reason and Emotion in Psychotherapy*. Revised and updated edition. New York: Birch Lane Press.

Ellis, A. (2002). *Overcoming Resistance: A Rational Emotive Behavior Therapy Integrated Approach*. 2nd edition. New York: Springer Publishing Co.

Ellis, A. and Becker, I. (1982) *A Guide to Personal Happiness*. North Hollywood, CA: Wilshire.

Ellis, A. and Bernard, M.E. (1985) 'What is rational-emotive therapy (RET)?', in A. Ellis and M.E. Bernard (eds), *Clinical Applications of Rational-Emotive Therapy*. New York: Plenum.

Ellis, A. and Dryden, W. (1997) *The Practice of Rational Emotive Behavior Therapy*. 2nd edition. New York: Springer.

Frisch, M.B. (1992) 'Use of the quality of life inventory in problem assessment and treatment planning for cognitive therapy of depression', in A. Freeman and F. M. Dattilio (eds), *Comprehensive Casebook of Cognitive Therapy*. New York: Plenum.

Gendlin, E.T. (1978) *Focusing*. New York: Everest House.

Grieger, R.M. and Boyd, J. (1980) *Rational-Emotive Therapy: A Skills-based Approach*. New York: Van Nostrand Reinhold.

Hauck, P. (1991) *Hold Your Head up High*. London: Sheldon Press.

Kelly, G.A. (1955) *The Psychology of Personal Constructs*. New York: Norton.

Lazarus, A.A. (1981) *The Practice of Multimodal Therapy*. New York: McGraw-Hill.

McKay, M., Davis, M. and Fanning, P. (1997) *Thoughts and Feelings: Taking Control of Your Moods and Your Life*. 2nd edition. Oakland, CA: New Harbinger Publications.

Mahoney, M.J. (1988) 'The cognitive sciences and psychotherapy: patterns in a developing relationship', in K.S. Dobson (ed.), *Handbook of Cognitive-Behavioral Therapies*. New York: Guilford.

Maultsby, M.C., Jr. (1984) *Rational Behavior Therapy*. Englewood Cliffs, NJ: Prentice-Hall.

Maultsby, M.C., Jr. and Ellis, A. (1974) *Techniques for Using Rational-Emotive Imagery*. New York: Institute for Rational-Emotive Therapy.

Neenan, M. and Dryden, W. (2000) *Essential Rational Emotive Behaviour Therapy*. London: Whurr.

Neenan, M. and Dryden, W. (2001) *Learning From Errors in Rational Emotive Behaviour Therapy*. London: Whurr.

Neenan, M. and Dryden, W. (2002) *Cognitive Behaviour Therapy: An A–Z of Persuasive Arguments*. London: Whurr.

Passons, W.R. (1975) *Gestalt Approaches in Counseling*. New York: Holt, Rinehart and Winston.

Persons, J.B. (1989) *Cognitive Therapy in Practice: A Case Formulation Approach*. New York: Norton.

Persons, J.B., Burns, D.D. and Perloff, J.M. (1988) 'Predictors of dropout and outcome in cognitive therapy for depression in a private practice setting', *Cognitive Therapy and Research*, 12: 557–75.

Rogers, C.R. (1957) 'The necessary and sufficient conditions of therapeutic personality change', *Journal of Consulting Psychology*, 21: 95–103.

Tracey, T.J. (1984) 'The stages of influence in counseling and psychotherapy', in F.J. Dorn (ed.), *The Social Influence Process in Counseling and Psychotherapy*. Springfield, IL: Charles C. Thomas.

Trexler, L.D. (1976) 'Frustration is a fact, not a feeling', *Rational Living*, 11(2): 19–22.

Walen, S. (2002) 'My idiosyncratic practice of REBT', in W. Dryden (ed.), *Idiosyncratic Rational Emotive Behaviour Therapy*. Ross-on-Wye: PCCS Books.

Walen, S.R., DiGiuseppe, R. and Dryden, W. (1992) *A Practitioner's Guide to Rational-Emotive Therapy*. 2nd edition. New York: Oxford University Press.

Yankura, J. and Dryden, W. (1994) *Albert Ellis*. London: Sage.

Index

DATE DUE

5/10/07			
APR 3 0 2007			
NOV 2 8 2007			
NOV 2 7 2007			
NOV 1 9 2008			
NOV 1 9 2008			
DEC 0 4 2011			
DEC 0 7 2011			
GAYLORD			PRINTED IN U.S.A.